PASTORS

A R E

PEOPLE

TOO

PASTORS

A R E

PEOPLE

TOO

DAVID B. BIEBEL
AND
HOWARD W.
LAWRENCE,

EDITORS

Regal Books

A Division of GL Publications
Ventura, California, U.S.A.

Rights for publishing this book in other languages are contracted by Gospel Literature International (GLINT) foundation. GLINT also provides technical help for the adaptation, translation, and publishing of Bible study resources and books in scores of languages worldwide. For further information, contact GLINT, Post Office Box 488, Rosemead, California 91770, U.S.A., or the publisher.

Published by Regal Books
A Division of GL Publications
Ventura, California 93006
Printed in U.S.A.

Library of Congress Cataloging in Publication Data

Pastors are people too.

    1. Clergy—Office—Case studies.   2. Pastoral theology—Case studies.   I. Biebel, David B.
II. Lawrence, Howard W., 1948-
BV660.2.P27   1986   253'.2'0926   86-3835
ISBN 0-8307-1102-3

Dedication

To the people we have been privileged to serve:
Sometimes in human weakness, ignorance or fear,
Sometimes in godly power, wisdom and creativity,
But always to the building of His Kingdom.

Contents

About the Contributors:

The following, listed alphabetically, have contributed chapters to this book. All are ordained ministers, holding the Doctor of Ministry degree, or are presently involved in a program leading to that degree. All are either graduates of or students at Gordon-Conwell Theological Seminary in South Hamilton, Massachusetts.

David B. Biebel

George H. Butler

James E. Collins

Robert A. DeLange

Ralph G. Eib with
Lynn Yoxtheimer Eib

Robert W. Goodwin

Joseph C. Hicks

Donald C. Hoagland

Howard W. Lawrence

Kenneth G. Lawrence

Eli R. Mercer

David M. Midwood

Kenneth E. Phelps

Introduction

The stories in this book are true! They are the down-to-earth, off-the-pedestal experiences of ordained ministers, whose combined years in ministry exceed 150. All of the contributors have earned doctorates or are students on the doctoral level, and all are or have been students at Gordon-Conwell Theological Seminary.

You won't find any ready-to-be-canonized saints in these pages either; just servants of the Lord. They're people that God has used in spite of—or sometimes, because of—the weaknesses that come from being human.

When we started working seriously on this book, we had in mind the title, "What You Always Needed to Know About the Ministry but Never Learned in Seminary." Our thesis was that sometimes God uses those in the ministry as He creatively empowers them to function as ministers in nontextbook situations. We issued an invitation to colleagues to contribute chapters describing experiences showing how the Lord prepared, equipped or taught them through their experiences to serve Him.

As the book took shape, we came to the conclusion that what we really have here is a book about life—God working in the lives of His servants and ministering through them to the lives of others. We deeply appreciate the honesty and transparency of our contributors, some of whom have provided intensely personal glimpses of God at work in their situations.

Because some of the accounts which follow are so personal, we have protected the confidentiality of the contributors and persons described by asking our contributors to change names or other data, as appropriate, though the accounts remain true. Also, we have listed contributors alphabetically at the outset, while not specifically identifying them with their chapters.

As we reflect on the message of this book, certain truths emerge. These truths apply not only to our fellow pastors and seminarians, but to Christians everywhere, since all believers are called to be ministers or servants of the One who redeemed them, in His grace, to be vehicles of that grace in the world.

One recurring theme is the personal discovery of how that grace is, indeed, sufficient to any time of need. Pastors have the privilege, as they serve the flock of God, of entering into the joys, struggles and sorrows of people of varying ages and situations in a brief span of time. The result is a certain intensity of life experience, with wide variety and potentiality, requiring the kind of creativity and flexibility that can come only as ministers of the faith learn to depend on His Spirit, the very source of creativity.

Also, the ability to minister effectively in a given setting quite often arises from an individual's personal history.

So, this book is not about supermen or spiritual giants, but about people who come to their task in weakness to find His power. They may approach it in brokenness, discovering a wholeness only He can bring. Perhaps they may even come in confusion, finding that peace which passes all comprehension, a peace that can provide a sure foundation for reaching out.

Thus, as the contributors present themselves in these pages, we expect that you will find yourself here, too. Perhaps you will laugh, or maybe you will cry, as you enter into this picture of life.

Finally, we trust that, having found yourself here, you will also find strength and hope as you may need it in your own situation. Specifically, we want you to see how God is available to help you become a person He can use in spite of, in the midst of or because of the story He's writing about you. For you are His book, known and read by others, a minister He would like to use to show others something of His love.

We will be gratified, and this project will be worthwhile, if you find through your reading a new sense of calling or purpose, even joy.

David B. Biebel
Howard W. Lawrence

Is It Okay to Pull the Plug?

What would you say to someone who is terminally ill and wants to end his life? Euthanasia, or mercy killing, is occurring in more and more hospitals every day. But is that an option for Christians? Is that an option for anyone, for that matter? Read how one pastor grapples with the delicate question, "Is it okay to pull the plug?"

The nurse had stepped out of the intensive care unit as I read to Joe the passage he had indicated he wished to hear, "I consider that our present sufferings are not worth comparing with the glory that will be revealed in us" (Rom. 8:18). As I continued, Joe turned and stared toward the corner of the room where the respirator mercilessly inflated his lungs. Reaching up to his mouth, he disconnected the respirator tube from the tube in his throat.

I paused and asked, "Do you want me to get that hooked up again?"

He shook his head, "No!"

I had felt a special leading to make that early morning visit to the city hospital. Joe was dying. Fully alert, he was on a respirator, being watched continuously. Because of our relationship, I knew what he needed to hear from Scripture. As he pointed to passages, I read them. As he tossed in pain, I prayed for his death.

Instead of the peaceful ticking of a grandfather clock in the familiar surrounding of home, Joe was forced to listen to the mechanical pumping of the respirator and to feel its rhythmic inflation of his chest. His pain became mine as I imagined myself in his situation. "This is no place to die," I thought, "but neither is it a place to live."

The medical people in charge gave him no hope of recovery, yet their monitors blinked and buzzed his vital signs, helpless to make things better, but ready to flash the worst when the inevitable took place. I asked myself what society has gained by replacing the scene of the family gathered at the deathbed of a loved one with the sterile, uncaring gadgets surrounding my parishioner.

I was angry. I remember reviewing the facts as I saw them. Here was a man ready to die, spiritually, emotionally and physically. He was terminal. The medical people expected his death at any moment. Why had they robbed him of the tremendous opportunity to share his dying thoughts, forcing him to communicate with his eyes and by nodding his head?

Not long after this incident, Joe's wife shared with me a note he had written during this time of physical suffering. It was a note to God, reflecting Joe's frustration:

I begged the doctors to stop. They were putting lines in, putting tubes through my nose, putting airway tubes down my throat and then an arterial line up from the groin to control my heart and on top of that, four IV [intravenous] lines, plus fluid restrictions. At this time they didn't know what they were going to do . . . Brothers and Sisters, I begged, yes, pleaded with God to die.

When Joe disconnected the respirator tube, I was left feeling literally paralyzed as a multitude of conflicting thoughts hit me. It was like viewing a fast-paced multimedia presentation with my thoughts being projected on a screen:

> At least I will be here when he dies, but I don't want to be here when he dies!
> I should call for the nurse immediately, but then she will just hook up the line and prolong the pain!

I suppose the most sobering thought arose from the circumstantial evidence. The nurse had heard me speak of the joy of heaven, of the opportunity to be free from pain and cumbersome tubes. She had seen Joe raise his finger heavenward when I spoke of the opportunity of going home. She had heard me express what I sensed Joe wanted to express concerning the frustration of not being able to communicate. Then, when she had left the room, the tube mysteriously came unhooked! I could see the headlines and hear myself pleading with a jury to believe that even though I had been asking God to take him home, I had not unhooked that tube!

A recent courtroom experience did nothing to calm my fears. I had gone there to provide moral support. As we waited for the case to be heard, I whispered to a lawyer next to me, "How long do you think it will be before my friend's case will be heard?"

His answer stuck with me, striking me as symptomatic of the judicial system. "You know," he said, "if you had asked me that when I first began my law practice, I could have told you almost exactly, but now that I have been watching what goes on in the courtroom for years, I can tell you with confidence, that I have no idea!"

My private multi-media presentation continued in my mind, and the more I saw, the more complex the issues became. Simple and obvious at first, the more I thought about the potentialities of this situation, the more I discovered new images complicating the scene, hidden images emerging from time to time as my ministry to Joe continued.

I found myself understanding Dr. C. Everett Koop's summary statement near the end of *The Right to Live The Right to Die:*

> Most of the dilemmas that present themselves in reference to the dying patient have been described. If the reader feels at this juncture that he does not have a good grasp on how the author would act in every imaginable circumstance, then the reader has grasped the situation rather well.[1]

It is one thing to enter the ministry with preconceived answers concerning euthanasia situations. Testing them in real life is quite another; the images seem far more complicated when facing the real thing.

My relationship with Joe had begun about four years prior to that early morning intensive care unit experience. Late one summer afternoon as I worked in the study, the phone rang. An unidentified caller, trying to disguise the fact that his question was about himself, asked, "If a person has been diagnosed with a terminal disease and has no hope of recovery, what difference would it make if he took his own life?"

My hands became sweaty; I felt a cold chill come over me as I realized the seriousness of this inquiry and sensed that the person in question was on the other end of the line. I fought to keep images of slit wrists, falls from high places and drug overdoses from clouding my mind. I admit I felt totally unprepared for that real-life question at that hour of the afternoon.

Probing for more information, I discovered that the man was, indeed, talking about himself. His reasons for suicide sounded very noble and legitimate. In his early 40s, he had been recently diagnosed as having severe coronary artery disease, which was inoperable, along with chronic kidney failure and diabetes.

The best he could hope for was a few months. He would never work again. The doctors warned that in his remaining time he would have some good days, but they would become fewer and the hospital stays more frequent. He had a wife and one daughter in her early teens.

With great emotion he said, "I just can't imagine putting my family through such an ordeal. To end it all right now really seems like the best thing to do for all concerned." Had I not been a Christian, what he said might have seemed just as sensible to me as it seemed to him.

However, I am a Christian, and I didn't know if he was.

This was the all-important question. If he was, we would have a shared philosophy of life, based on Scripture. If not, I would have a more difficult time showing him why mercy killing is unacceptable.

I probed for more information, "I need to know a little more about you, particularly about your understanding of God. I would like to ask you a couple of questions about it if I could."

He encouraged me to continue. "Have you come to the point in your spiritual life," I asked, "where you know for certain that if you were to die today, you would go to heaven?"

"I think I would," he said, "but I am not certain what would happen if I killed myself."

That was one time when I wished I had a different perspective on suicide, one teaching that not only is suicide wrong, but that it is unforgivable and its judgment deserving of hell. My own convictions weren't that dogmatic, but I didn't know where this man stood. Here was another dilemma. If the fear of eternal punishment because of suicide was the only thing keeping him from taking his own life, I didn't want to be guilty of encouraging him by removing that fear!

I asked another question, "Suppose you were to stand before God right now and He were to say to you, 'Why should I let you into heaven?' What would you say?"

This time he answered with certainty, "Because I have asked Jesus Christ to enter my life and forgive me, and I trust Him for my salvation."

Now things were on firmer ground. "If you have committed yourself to Christ, " I said, "then your life is no longer your own. By His death on the cross, He paid the price for your life and when you came to believe He was the Messiah, the Christ, then you also were telling Him that you would be His servant. Your life is no longer yours to take."

He thanked me and hung up.

As I placed the phone on the receiver, I was overwhelmed by the implications of what I had just said. I had just told someone that because of his faith, he could not take the easy way out of the situation and that because of his faith in Christ, the one solution that seemed so simple and merciful to all concerned was no longer an option. The whole conversation had lasted no longer than 10 minutes and I still had no idea who the caller was or whether he would be taking my advice.

Months later, I met Joe after one of our morning worship services. He identified himself as that caller and thanked me for giving him the courage to continue on. I was more thankful to meet him than he will ever know, since shortly after that conversation, there had been a suicide in a nearby town and I wondered if I was in some way responsible. Meeting Joe put that fear to rest.

By the time Joe started attending church with his family, his stays in the hospital's intensive care unit were becoming more frequent. Each time, the medical people would shrug their shoulders if asked whether or not he would survive, and then again when asked how much longer he might live.

More of those hidden images were emerging. My neat philosophical answer to Joe about belonging to God and therefore not having any right to take his own life took on added dimensions as his illness progressed.

One of the fundamental issues was the meaning of life itself. It's one thing to talk about life with someone just fired from a job, but quite another to discuss it with someone connected to a life-support system. It's one thing to tell a relatively mobile, alert, contributing member of society not to give up on a nice summer afternoon. It's quite another to see him, early in the morning, four years later, unhooking his respirator tube and feeling he had a right to do so, with God's blessing.

But was it really different? How is life defined anyhow? I was learning how terribly inadequate the medical definition "brain dead" really was. At the same time, however, a theological definition of death can be equally inadequate.

We can determine biblically what it means to be fully alive as a human being. The Word of God shows persons alive as capable of relationships, choices, moral judgments, productivity and, of course, an ability to relate to God. However, the fall of mankind (Gen. 3) initiated the fulfillment of God's promise: "In the day that you eat from it you shall surely die" (Gen. 2:17, *NASB*). Since that fateful day in Eden, creation has been in the process of groaning, and mankind has been involved in the process of dying while still alive.

My understanding is that life begins when, by God's grace, His Spirit enters into an individual's heart through faith. Life then is realized in Christ, and physical death only means to bring about the completeness of that life. Even we who are alive in Christ are physically dying and, in fact, must physically die to truly live. Therefore, it should not fall to the theologian to decide when a person is "dead" and the plug can be pulled. Actually, both medical and theological definitions are necessary, but both fall short of defining death since both have a purpose to speak of "life".

In his struggle, Joe began to focus on Paul's testimony and to make it his own, "For to me, to live is Christ, and to die is gain" (Phil. 1:21, *NASB*). He was learning that life is not so much situations or productivity; it is a relationship with Christ. Here, the image of life's definition was sharpened for me. There was a great difference between Joe's initial desire to take his own life, escaping what God had planned, and the peace with God which prompted him to unhook the respirator, looking toward heaven with a conviction that his work on earth was completed.

The issue is entirely different for a terminally ill person who has made no profession of faith in Christ. In that case, death would bring something quite opposite from relief, in terms of eternity.

Thankfully, Joe knew the true source of life, and he was willing to live as a servant of Christ, no matter what the circumstances.

Another of the hidden images this experience brought into focus was the matter of intent in euthanasia. An Anglican pamphlet entitled, "On Dying Well," expresses it this way:

> There is a clear distinction to be drawn between rendering someone unconscious at the risk of killing him and killing him in order to render him unconscious. . . . There is a decisive difference between the situation of a medical practitioner whose patient dies as the result of an increased dosage of a pain-killing drug and who would use a safer drug had it been available, and that of a public executioner in states which employ this means of carrying out the death penalty who chooses drugs for their death-inducing properties. Two rivers may take their rise at a very little distance from one another on a mountainous

> plateau, but this slight difference may deter-
> mine that the one flows north and the other
> south.[2]

Sitting next to Joe's bed that Monday morning, I perceived that his original intent—to take his own life in order
to escape physical and emotional pain—had changed. His
decision to unhook the tube was not an act of suicide or
escape, but a willful intent to let God be God.

My paralysis in that situation was also caused by that
same desire. It was not my intent that he should be killed
or left to die, but that Joe be allowed to die with dignity.
This was clearly not an act of suicide or euthanasia, but an
act that allowed God to be God.

But then another hidden image appeared, for although
Joe's action was clearly not suicidal, my perspective on
that question might not be shared by others. More frightening still, how would anyone else know my own lack of
action was not a wrongful act of mercy killing? At that
moment, however, the important thing for me was that I
knew the difference—and that Joe knew the difference.
Also, I knew that his family would understand.

This understanding was another of the hidden images
which had become increasingly clear as Joe's situation
worsened. In fact, it had been his concern to spare his
family the grief of living with his illness that had prompted
Joe's initial phone call.

His illness affected everyone close to him. Joe's grief
became their grief; his frustration became their frustration. When he would become deeply depressed, those
close to him would search for ways to lift him up. Following one of his critical episodes, Joe's wife protested, "I
don't know how much more of this I can take. Sometimes I

feel like it would be much easier if he would die so we could get on with life here on earth."

I appreciated her honesty. After many trips to the hospital, I sometimes discovered I was feeling the same way. Euthanasia would have been an act of mercy for close friends as well, wouldn't it?

At this point, I began to see that just as the terminally ill person must base his life not on circumstances but on a relationship with Christ, so must those experiencing the illness with him. We cannot eliminate suffering, nor should our goal be to escape situations we do not enjoy. Just as it must be the goal of the terminal patient to press on by sharing Paul's testimony, "For to me, to live is Christ," so must the same be the goal of all who share his emotional pain.

Joe's wife pointed out to me the value of a ministry which both supported and encouraged Joe, while standing with his family and friends, who in a very real way felt themselves dying with him.

It became obvious to me that here was not just an individual in a textbook-type situation, but a man who was a part of all of us. Sensing God in the center of our situation, we began to trust Him. It was no longer a matter of an individual ruining an otherwise good day, but a matter of questioning, "How today, God, do you want me to serve you in this?" This refocusing of our thoughts and affirmation of togetherness unleashed a spirit of ministry to a degree I had not experienced before. We were beginning to sense the mercy of God together.

The final hidden image, and in retrospect the most significant to me, was the hand of God in Joe's life. Although he had been given as little as four months to live, Joe had been allowed four years. During that time he was on the

critical list numerous times, and each time medicine did
what it could to prolong his life. Time and again though, it
was the Lord who received the credit when Joe recovered.

Looking back, I'm grateful that on that Monday morning I wasn't in charge. Nor was Joe. While I sat paralyzed
in my thoughts, the nurse returned and routinely rein-
serted the tube. I was not accused, and Joe did not die.
Again, he began miraculously improving.

One day later, the respirator was removed. Two days
later, he underwent additional cardiac testing which led to
successful bypass surgery by the end of the week. Immediately after that surgery, Joe's kidneys began functioning
again and he was given a new lease on life.

My anger with medical people who refused to give up
on a person labeled "hopeless" changed to appreciation.
As Thomas Elkins affirms, certain medical values have
been undeniable through the centuries:

> One is that medicine has had a radically positive
> view of man. Man is worth saving, is worth
> treating. He is worth enough to have other men
> and women—doctors—work night after night
> away from their families and in the constant
> threat of malpractice suits.[3]

After Joe had recovered from the bypass surgery, we
talked about the incident with the respirator tube. We both
admitted we had been humbled by it before God. It wasn't
so much that we felt we had done something wrong, but
that God had overruled even when the situation seemed
hopeless. We were humbled by our inability to know, yet

pleased that God had asked that we only be submissive to His will and open to His plan.

Following his heart surgery, Joe had a radiant testimony for all to see and hear, although he spent much time hospitalized with complications from his diabetes. It was a difficult time for him and his family, but a time of learning what Paul meant when he said, "For to me, to live is Christ."

Joe was able to return home, becoming actively involved in the church's ministry, even returning to work. He was ready to live and he was ready to die; he was ready to be a servant of his Lord.

It surprised us all when Joe did enter into the presence of Christ almost five years after the doctors gave him no hope. He had returned home after church, not feeling well. This time there were no tubes and no decisions to be made about prolonging his life. He had completed the task God had given him to do. In the process, he had helped me see some of the hidden images in what I had thought was a relatively simple picture—teaching me humbly before God to seek His wisdom in all things.

In one of his darkest nights, Joe had written a letter to God, part of which follows. Alone, with machines at his side, he wrote:

> Whatever happens, God is in complete control of my life. I have failed Him before and probably will again and I ask His mighty forgiveness. But I also want all to know that it was each and every one who visited and prayed with me that got me through.
>
> I can truly feel Jesus' arms holding me close like a brother. I have always said things can get

worse, but when God's arms are about you, be human, be scared, be afraid, but brother, trust God for all He is worth, He really cares and loves you. I am here because of His love and care. Besides, as I said before, He doesn't want me up there one minute sooner than He has to have me. He has got something better for me to do down here.

> Thanks God,
> All My Love,
> Your servant, Joe

How Do *You* Identify?

Do you have a "Joe" in your life? How many "Joes" are there right now in your church? They may not be hooked up to respirators or other life-support systems in the Intensive Care Unit of your local hospital, but someday soon they will be. How many people in your Sunday School class or fellowship group will be visiting the doctor in the next few weeks for a routine check-up and will hear the dreaded words, "You have cancer"? It happens, and someday soon you, your pastor or one of your deacons will be standing beside the hospital bed of your own "Joe."

The most important issue you may have to deal with may not be whether or not it's okay to pull the plug, but rather how you and your church will react to "Joe." That's a question we all would do well to struggle with, because how we react will determine whether or not we will ever have an effective ministry with Joe in his critical time of physical and spiritual need. Joe may soon be "cut off" from the rest of the Body of Christ by death; let us not be guilty of cutting him off from the Body by our neglect to minister and care for him when he needs his church the most.

First of all, it would be wise for us to consider the fact that not all members of the Body are gifted for visiting and physically caring for others who are wired together by tubes and fed by miles of IVs. More than one young seminary student has been called out of a career in pastoral ministry and led into counseling because they found it difficult to remain conscious in the presence of a slow-drip IV and a pint of blood hanging over the patient's bed. Some pastors find they can visit a patient in the hospital, but never just after lunch. Some find they are absolutely worthless in a medical crisis.

You may be different, however. And your visit, your very presence at the bedside of a terminally-ill or recovering member of your church fellowship may be worth more than anything doctors could do to lift one's spirit. If God has gifted you for this kind of ministry, your church will benefit all the more as you put that gift into service.

Second, if you find that your gifts for ministry do not include routine visitation to the bedsides of the "Joes" of your church, you can serve the members of the Body in other meaningful ways. The spirits of a number of hospitalized believers have been encouraged and strengthened because their brothers and sisters in the Lord were gifted in other ministries of caring.

For example, it is hard to imagine the difference it makes in one's spirit to see a mailbox full of cards and letters; it sounds so simple, so easy, and yet it is so effective and so meaningful. Have you ever noticed how bright and cheerful a hospital room full of cards and flowers is compared to one that is bleak and empty? One is full of expressions of love and joy, the other a reminder that no one really cares, or knows how to express concern. If you can't visit "Joe" in the hospital, send a card. Joe will get the message. In his time of need, someone who is part of the Body of Christ remembered him, and that carries with it some very important therapy in itself.

Finally, let us remember Joe's own words, "Whatever happens, God is in complete control of my life." Christians have been called to serve one another in times of need, and in many instances we will set out to minister in situations for which we have never been, nor ever will be, trained. Just as God is in control of Joe's life, we can be assured that He is in control of ours as well. As we seek to serve His family in ways we might feel at a loss or ill at ease, let us turn each visit and call over to His leading and allow the Great Physician to minister to and through each one of us.

2

One Flew Over the Church's Nest

What does the term *mentally ill* make you think of? Whatever comes to your mind, it is important to remember that God loves the mentally ill as much as He loves you and me. This is the story of how one pastor came to realize that through God's love, he was able to accept and deal with the mental illness of one of his parishioners, and in the process, learn some very valuable lessons for developing a significant ministry.

Two men in white coats were running behind me while Stan's wife patiently waited for another adventure to be over. It was a warm summer day, and I found myself chasing my friend and parishioner down a hillside in order to get him back into the state hospital where he needed to be. I told the two men to back off, that Stan would be alright if they would just give me a minute to calm him down.

Stan had been in the process of being admitted voluntarily to the hospital when the person filling out the admitting forms became too demanding of details. Stan snapped, ran out the door and started down that grassy knoll in search of freedom and perspective. Eventually, the two men stood motionless at the top of the hill, Stan stopped running and the two of us talked for what seemed an eternity to those waiting above.

As we walked back to the hospital, Stan crept up the hill like a wounded animal, fully aware that the time ahead would be unpleasant. It would flood his mind, his entire being with years of painful memories.

Together we filled out the remaining paperwork, he was admitted and the same two men in white coats led him beyond steel doors that Stan knew only too well. Just before he went through those doors, he smiled at me and said, "Thanks for seeing me through this. You and I both know I need to be here for awhile."

Tears filled his wife's eyes and mine, as we walked to the car to return home. Stan had become increasingly out of control in the past couple of weeks, and all three of us knew he could not stay at home any longer. This was a scenario that had occurred many times.

My ministry with Stan, over a period of five years, was one of maintenance. There is little hope of his becoming an independent person again, yet he has accomplished things and witnessed dimensions of life that few who are "whole" will ever know or could ever cope with in their daily living.

When I first met Stan, I was just four months out of seminary, confident that I was prepared to handle most pastoral situations. But I wasn't really prepared to deal with someone so irrational, so mean at times and so loving at other times. It was only as I learned to come alongside Stan without a lot of pat answers and preconceived ideas that I began to have an effective ministry with him.

What follows is a segment of a story that Stan started about himself, but never finished. It is included here with his permission, and in the hope that the reader will recognize the individuality of every person, though some may be more "different" than others. Everyone is a child of God, and each stands in need of pastoral care, regardless of those differences.

IN THE BEGINNING

May 8, 1951: It was a beautiful day in May. A friend of mine . . . asked me if I would like to take a ride . . . . I didn't know which direction I was going or where I was heading. I WAS MANIC! Then we arrived at our destination, which was the door to the "Admission Suite" of State Hospital. Inside the door at a very nice desk sat Dr. Berg. He was considered the best psychiatrist in the area.

After talking to him for 15 minutes, he nodded his head, knocked on the door and two very large attendants escorted me into a tile bathroom. They told me to disrobe and take a shower. When my shower was completed, I was escorted directly to a four-foot by eight-foot solid concrete room. Four concrete walls, a concrete floor, a concrete ceiling and a window with extra-duty wire mesh screen that was encased in a metal frame that had to be opened with a key. Behind the window was a conventional window with unbreakable glass in a heavy-duty black window frame. There was no bed, no bathroom, no bureau—NOTHING BUT EMPTINESS.

There was a three-inch solid oak door, which was locked with a slide bolt and an extra heavy-duty lock. In addition there was another lock that was locked with an old-fashioned straight key. There was a rectangular hole cut in the door, not large enough to put your head through, and that was your only ventilation. THAT WAS MY HOME AWAY FROM HOME! AND I HATED IT!

May 9, 1951: My wife signed commitment papers. They had to be signed by Dr. Berg and our family doctor, Dr. Blake, because it required two doctors in 1951 to have a patient committed. She went to the State Hospital and got the affidavit at the courthouse and left the papers at the Administration Building. At the Admissions Building she received my wallet and my ring from the nurse on duty.

May 14, 1951: My wife received a telegram from the hospital because my doctor had not received my commitment papers.

May 15, 1951: My wife made an appointment to come into the hospital after she finished teaching school, to sign papers to begin my shock treatments. My wife talked with Dr. Kislin while she was at the hospital.

He said I had been hyperactive, figuring
lengths and squares on the wall, pounding
on the wall, talking constantly, and denuded
myself and [I was] put in seclusion. I stayed
dressed for two days, but I was back in
seclusion again the third day. I ate well after
not liking the tube-feeding. My health was
checked and found to be in excellent condition. My heart, my spinal cord, my nerves
and my muscles. I kidded Dr. Kislin, knew
everyone and remembered everything.

May 16, 1951: I was taken to the
Medical-Surgical Building with two attendants in a hospital car for my pre-shock
workup. This consisted of a complete back
x-ray and an electrocardiogram, better
known as EKG.

May 17, 1951: Shock treatments begin. I
was taken from my room, after having my
temperature taken rectally, my blood pressure, and my pulse. Twenty minutes
(approximately) before the treatment, a
nurse gave me an injection in the arm to
make my mouth dry. I was first for shock. I'll
never forget it. I was led to the day hall,
which had windows covered with sheets,
and there were six attendants, a nurse and a
doctor. In 1951 there was no Sodium Pento-
thal to inject intravenously to make you
unconscious first. The electrodes were
strapped to your head, one on each side
and the leather strap was buckled in front.
The nurse inserted a round piece of filled

gauze, circular in nature, and she said, "Bite" and you were ZONKED!!! There was a litter on wheels adjacent to the shock table. As soon as your treatment was completed, the attendants rolled you from the table to the litter and wheeled you to the dormitory in the back and placed you on a bed. Approximately 20 minutes later you were awakened and told to come into the day hall. By then the shock table ("Buzz Box" as it was called) treatments were completed for everyone scheduled and you had coffee and toast. That was your breakfast.

SECLUSION IS HELL

Every morning after the routine duties were taken care of, I was let out of my side room and taken to the bathroom for a shower. I always felt it was my behavior at this time that would determine whether I would remain in my side room for another 24 hours or they would try me in the day hall with the other patients where I would have friends to communicate with. Every evening between eight and nine, a registered nurse would come into my seclusion room and give me an injection in the buttocks of sodium amytal, to help me sleep. I nick-named this "Blue Heaven." Sodium amytal was a remarkable medication, because in a short period of time you went off into a very

restful sleep. Every morning I was awakened at daybreak by the loud "Caw, Caw,
Caw" of the crows. It was heartwarming to
hear this, followed by the beautiful song of
the song sparrows—this was approximately
5 A.M. Since I had taken vocal lessons in college, I repeatedly sang "The Lord's Prayer." I
did this, hoping the Lord would intervene
and I would not get SHOCK!!!"

Stan received several more shock treatments after the
initial ones he wrote about. Fortunately, however, in
recent years, his medical care no longer requires shock
treatments. Today, the remembrance of them continues to
be a source of pain and fear that Stan will never forget.

When I first met Stan in 1978, he had been through a
myriad of life experiences. Suffice to say during that time
he was in and out of various state mental hospitals and
care facilities. There were periods of time when he was
able to function normally and hold down some nonpressure
jobs, and live a fairly regular life at home with his wife and
children. Since the mid-'70s the condition of his mental
state has grown somewhat worse. When he is home,
which is not as often as it was in the past, he is just about
able to see to his own needs. The day I first met Stan he
was hospitalized. As I was introduced to him, his first
words to me were, "Well, what do we have here?" followed by a few expletives. That was the beginning of our
relationship together.

Stan is a gentleman in his 50s with a big smile and a
warm heart. He taught me a great deal about what it is like
to carry the stigma of being mentally handicapped, and

how I, as a minister, could be of best service to people in his position.

I'll never forget the first lesson he taught me, which is that unless we have been through the kind of dehumanizing that Stan has been through in various institutions, we can't comprehend or totally empathize with the person to whom we are trying to minister.

Since first meeting Stan, I had visited with him three or four times, and things were going pretty well—or so I thought. Walking into the dayroom at the state hospital one crisp autumn day, I felt confident that my visit with Stan would be a blessing for both of us.

"Hello, Stan," I said, as I casually walked over to the chair where he was sitting. "How are you today?" I questioned.

"I don't want to see you. Get the hell out of here—*now*, Rev!" he exclaimed.

How could he do that to me? We were going to have a good visit together, or so I had planned. I had driven quite some distance to see him, and now he tells me to get lost. My ministerial-ego balloon burst, and I felt a sense of personal defeat as I walked out of the room and back to my car. Seminary had prepared me with advice as to what side of a patient's bed to sit on at the hospital, with Scripture texts to use in various situations and with an occasional warning to expect the unexpected, but not with instructions on what to do when told to get lost.

During the next two weeks, as I went about my work, I occasionally thought about my encounter with Stan. Questions came to mind like: How do I get the motivation to go back into the 'lion's den'? How do I cope with my own feeling of rejection so that I can minister effectively? What will I do if it happens again?

However, after prayer—and, I know now, the Holy Spirit's leading—I returned to the state hospital to visit Stan. Walking into the same room, I found him drinking a cup of coffee.

"Hi, Stan," I began, "how are you doing today?"

"Hi, Rev," he replied, with a smile, "I see you passed the test."

"What test was that?" I asked, with a puzzled countenance upon my face.

"Oh, the one I put you through the last time you were here to see what you were made of, Rev," he said. "I told you to 'get lost,' because I wanted to see whether you cared enough to come back or whether you would forget all about me," he said. "I liked you the first time we met, but I didn't know if I could trust you! There are a lot of people who have let me down in the past, and I wanted to see if you were a friend or a fly-by-night," he responded.

From that moment on, the windows opened wider on our relationship, and I indeed had a friend and a teacher who happened to have mental problems. Stan started to gain more control in ensuing days, and he was released from the hospital to be at home again.

Periodically, I began to visit him at home. As time went on, he began to open up to me about different aspects of his life—his illness, his family, his personal history, his spiritual state. All of that began to happen, not because I possessed some great theological insight, psychological astuteness or pastoral know-how, but because I made a conscious decision to come alongside and try my best to understand him.

Stan gave me insight into the deep sensitivity and good manners that people who have a mental problem usually possess. Often those who minister fail to see that aspect in them, because we are also aware of how "crazy" they can be and how out-of-touch they are with reality at times. Looking for all of those manifestations of various behavior patterns we read about in school, we can easily fall into the trap of analyzing rather than pastoring.

Arriving at Stan's house during his times of clarity was always a treat. He treated me with respect and dignity because I was his pastor. Some of that surely was due to his upbringing, but some of that I discovered was also true of many of his friends to whom I was introduced during his stays at the state hospital. I found it more than curious that some "normal" parishioners treat new pastors as though they are "wet behind the ears," while Stan and many others who share his condition found age or experience to be no barrier whatsoever.

Helping Stan grow in faith has been my greatest reward in working with him—and a constant challenge. He had been raised in a church environment, and had some familiarity with Scripture. Since his hospitalization in 1951, his church attendance has been sporadic. He was embarrassed about his condition and never wanted to risk embarrassing his wife publicly. Also, during the '70s, as he spent more and more time in hospitals, he became angry at God and resentful of the institutional Church and its inability to assist someone like himself. Unfortunately, regarding the Church, he was correct, for the Church had not done as much as it could have to help him.

As my relationship with Stan grew, he began to talk about spiritual things and about going to church. He had all sorts of theological questions. During his moments of rationality, some of those questions were profound. Stan is really a very brilliant man who happens to have moments of irrationality.

One of these moments occurred on a Sunday morning. While leading worship, I happened to glance out the sanctuary window just in time to see someone swinging a golf club, hitting golf balls on the strip of grass next to the wall of the sanctuary. The familiar orange baseball cap told me it was Stan!

After worship, I discovered he had come to church with his wife, but had decided at the last moment to wait in the car because he wasn't feeling well. That Sunday would have been his second time in worship in years. Afterwards, we discovered he had brought golf clubs along because he wanted to play golf with us.

So, after the service, still in our robes, the other pastor and I took a few minutes to hit some golf balls with Stan on the church grass, as he talked with us. Little did we realize how spiritually therapeutic those few moments would be for Stan.

He reminded me that a week earlier I had shown up at his door in "loud" green slacks, because I was planning to play golf later that day. Stan had wanted to play, too—desperately so—because golfing represented the freedom to do what other people could do, especially what I was going to do that day. Although he hadn't said anything about it then, he was now delivering his message to us outside the church after that service.

Spending those few moments with Stan hitting golf balls in clerical garb paid some great dividends. Two people, who in his mind represented God's love, the Church—the whole ball of wax—took time to meet his needs. The next time I saw him he handed me the following poem he had written:

JESUS

I believe Someone in the great somewhere,
Now I know the power of prayer.
There was a man they called a Saviour;
Now I know He controls behavior.
His name was Jesus, He was quite a man,
He healed the sick, walked across miles of
    sand,
Just to show his love for every man.
But it took two friends of mine,
Brotherhood is being kind.
This is something I searched to find,
Now at last I've peace of mind.
But it took two men we know—
These two guys they had to show
This stubborn man on earth below
His faith would grow from day to day
When on his knees he'd pray and pray,
And in his heart he'd yield the right of way
To an even greater Man above
Who shared with all the world His almighty
    love.
Now I believe.

This simple, lovely poem and that simply laughable situation on the church lawn marked the awakening of Stan's spiritual life. His commitment to Christ was real; he knew it, and so did I. All of the other "stuff" that had gone on in his life seemed insignificant because, regardless of what lay ahead, he was spiritually whole and secure.

A few months later Stan was in the hospital again. This time it was a city hospital with a well-known reputation for treating psychiatric problems. Stan had managed to get himself in isolation. He had broken the jaw of an attendant in a fit of anger and injured his own hand and arm in the process.

When I was able to see him again he had changed drastically. The merry Stan that had been hitting golf balls along the sanctuary wall weeks earlier had become the highly-sedated patient who demonstrated a broken spirit. The physician treating him revealed to me that the dosage of medication he was on would normally be too much for a horse, let alone a human being, but Stan had developed such a tolerance level over the years that he required more medication than the average patient.

Nothing could have adequately prepared me for the Stan I would see that day, but somewhere in my mind and heart I kept hearing the words of Jesus in Matthew 25:35-36: "For I was hungry and you gave me something to eat, I was thirsty and you gave me something to drink, I was a stranger and you invited me in, I needed clothes and you clothed me, I was sick and you looked after me, I was in prison and you came to visit me."

Later that day, during the visit with Stan, something interesting took place. Just about the time I was ready to leave, an alarm went off; there was a bomb scare in the hospital. The rule in the hospital was when an alarm went off, anyone visiting on a locked ward had to remain there until everything was checked out. It was another one of those "little lessons" that you pick up along the way. What was both fascinating and frightening during that experience was the radical change in behavior that takes place in patients when an alarm goes off. All of us are startled by alarms that signify danger, but patients in Stan's setting sometime become extremely nervous. Stan, who was more subdued than some of the other patients because of his high degree of medication, asked me to stand close to him while the attendants got everyone calmed down.

Minutes later the threat of a bomb going off was over, the alarm was turned off and I was ready to leave the hospital. Just the look on Stan's face as I left was a strong confirmation that my ministry during those hectic 10 minutes and my visitation that day meant a great deal to him. I felt very good about my calling as a minister that day, and it wasn't because I had preached an exciting three-point sermon or led a terrific Bible study. It was because, having put myself in a position of availability, the Holy Spirit used me and that particular situation to demonstrate God's love, in a very real and quiet way to a deserving person.

I owe much to Stan, my brother in Christ, who has allowed me to make mistakes. Stan allowed me to learn lessons that can't be learned in a classroom or a textbook. So often his own determination and spiritual sensitivity allowed me to think I was the teacher when on a number of occasions I was clearly the student.

It was a great joy for me to play a part in Stan's spiritual pilgrimage, to watch him take hold of the healing power of Christ, which in his case was not intended to make him psychologically whole, but spiritually whole. So many of my preconceived ideas about the mentally ill fell by the wayside during my ministry with Stan. I thank him for providing an important segment of my educational process outside the classroom and, of course, for being my friend.

A few days before I left the church where Stan is a member to accept a new charge, Stan handed me the following:

Please remember me with smile and laughter
When the Lord gives me His beckoned call
Because if you can only remember me with
    tears and sadness
Please do not remember me at all
                          Stan

How Do *You* Identify?

Sharing with someone like Stan can teach us some very valuable lessons about how to minister to a specific group of people with very special needs. Words like compassion, consistency, availability, patience, empathy and sincerity all apply to the kind of attitude that is necessary to have an effective ministry with the person suffering from a brain disease. These qualities tend to evolve in the process of ministry. If they don't, it may be that we're only going through the motions.

Stan and others who have been through his experience have a keen ability to know when we are being genuine and when we are not. Bear in mind that patients with a mental illness who have played all the necessary "games" and jumped through all the necessary institutional "hoops" are pretty astute at knowing whether someone is giving them their undivided attention or giving them a pastoral snow job.

So, first remember this: Persons with a serious chronic mental problem are not necessarily ignorant, unknowing or less intelligent than the person who is trying to minister to them. As one doctor stressed to the Hinckleys, parents of the schizophrenic young man who attempted to assassinate President Reagan, "It [mental illness] doesn't mean stupid."

Second, it is also important to remember that if we have a ministry with a mentally ill person, we have been blessed by God. For we have an opportunity to learn to depend on God's help and the inner strength He gives rather than on personal knowledge and abilities.

When we do come to grips with the fact that this special person we are working with—who at times may curse us, insult us and ridicule us—is a child of God just like us, then we are in a position to do significant ministry with that individual. At the seminary level we sometimes assume that everyone will like us or that everyone will at least listen to us.

Sometimes the mentally ill, as with those suffering from any other illness, are in need of what we have to say; at other times saying nothing is far better. At times they simply need our presence more than a mouthful of words. The writer of Ecclesiastes reminds us there is a time for everything—a time to embrace and a time to refrain, a time to be silent and a time to speak (see Eccles. 3). May God help us to keep our mouths shut at the right time.

3

When the Fleece Is
Barely Damp!

Do you struggle to be in God's will for your life?
How do you know what God will is for you?
Have you ever thrown out a "fleece"? Read
how one pastor deals with all of these questions
as he shares the experiences of candidating and
answering "the call" to another pastorate.

It *had* to be God's will. The coincidence was just too
striking. There my wife and I were in another state under-
going career counseling, attempting to get direction and
be refreshed from the discouragement we were feeling in
my first pastorate, when the kitchen telephone rang. The
pastor with whom we were staying answered and after a
few seconds told the caller he definitely wasn't interested.
Probably a life insurance salesman my wife mused.

"There's someone else here who might be interested," we heard our pastor friend telling the caller. Covering the receiver with his hand he announced in a loud whisper, "It's a pulpit committee chairman in Vermont. He was interested in me and my style of ministry. I told him I'm not looking to move, but that there was someone else here who might be interested. Do you want to talk to him?"

I was flabbergasted to say the least. Yes, I was discouraged after only a year in my first pastorate and even had guilty dreams about moving on, but I certainly wasn't pursuing another call. Then again, what harm could talking do? I hesitated, then picked up the receiver.

That was the beginning of a journey I was to take several more times over the next few years in the ministry— the quest to know when God is truly calling.

Before I finish telling what happened with that "coincidental" phone call, let me say this is not a chapter containing a magic formula for determining God's will. Neither is it a how-to manual for candidating pastors or searching churches. It *is* a glimpse into the feelings of a candidating pastor and a record of some of the guiding principles I've gleaned through my experiences with pulpit committees. I hope that it will begin to answer for both pastor and church that nagging question: "Is that really you, Lord?"

Remember poor Gideon who had trouble trusting God; God said He would save Israel by Gideon's hand. Gideon kept asking for one more sign so he could be really sure it was the Lord talking. First, he put out a wool fleece and asked that the dew be only on the fleece and not on the ground. The next morning it happened just as he asked and he wrung a bowlful of dew out of the fleece, Scripture says in Judges 6:37-40. But, Gideon still wasn't quite positive, so he asked that the next day the fleece be dry and the ground wet with dew. Again it happened as Gideon had requested and this time he was convinced that God's favor was truly with him.

I've sympathized with Gideon many times since I began searching for God's call in the pastoral ministry more than a decade ago. Sometimes I've desperately wanted to put out a fleece but thought better of the notion. Other times I've reluctantly set one out only to find it was barely damp instead of wringing wet with a bowlful of water! It is just those kinds of confusing situations I'd like to address as I consider the complex process and almost frightening responsibility of a church calling God's person to be it's pastor and of the pastor hearing God's call and answering.

Back to that coincidental phone call. After talking with the pulpit committee chairman, my wife and I decided to meet with them the next day and see if, indeed, the Lord might be calling us together. As we soon found out, that was easier said than done. We had candidated at only one church for our first pastorate. They liked us; we liked them. They called; we accepted on the spot. No doubts and no fleeces. We had been there a little more than a year now and even though the proverbial honeymoon was long over, somehow just this little meeting with a pulpit committee made us both uneasy—almost as if we were having an "affair" with another church!

For a pastor with any amount of integrity, looking for a new call while still in a present situation is a most frustrating time. Normally accustomed to dealing with the flock with honesty and openness, the searching pastor must resort to secrecy and sometimes downright deception in order to get away for the candidating process. There is always that lurking fear that the church might find out you are looking and then your leadership ability and ministry with them will be hampered or even finished. This unwanted shroud of secrecy hardly seems proper or Christlike when one is seeking God's leading.

How much better it would be to be able to share feelings and intentions and together as pastor and people seek and pray for God's guidance. I once heard another pastor explain his method of candidating by saying he went to a few trusted people in his present church and posed the question: "Do you think it's time for me to leave?" This up front honesty certainly seems to be in keeping with the Bible's view of the church as a family. It would also eliminate many guilt feelings and uneasiness experienced by the candidating pastor.

My wife and I returned to our first church from that short meeting with the Vermont pulpit committee feeling a little "dirty"—like we had flirted with a stranger when our spouse wasn't looking. It comforted us to know we hadn't gone away *looking* for a new call.

After that brief encounter, we both still had no clear idea of whether God was calling us to this new situation, but the coincidence of just happening to be in the right state, in the right house, at the right time, for the right phone call was so overwhelming, we decided the Spirit must be leading, and we would continue to pursue it. We agreed to have the church fly us back the next month to meet with various committees and preach a candidating sermon before the congregation. In the meantime we began to wait for God to tell us what to do. He didn't.

Don't get me wrong; many times my wife or I have felt God speaking or leading us in a certain direction and this time we simply wanted Him to say, "Yes, go to Vermont" or "No, don't go to Vermont." He did neither. The more we prayed, the more we realized how uncertain we were whether this move was our desire or the Lord's desire. It also didn't help any that there was a considerable salary increase involved and that the beautiful parsonage was brand new and idly waiting for the new pastoral family to pick out wallpaper and paint colors!

My wife and I began to feel that we were going to put a lot of stock in what took place during our candidating weekend. We went so far as to make it clear to the pulpit committee that we wanted to have the option to turn down a call should they issue us one and we felt it was not God's leading. We also gave them the same option of "turning us down," if they felt after closer scrutiny that I was not the pastor to whom God was leading them.

This might sound so logical it would be ludicrous to even have to mention, but there seems to be an unwritten rule for many churches and candidating pastors that once the level of official candidating is reached, the call is simply assumed and the yes answer merely expected. I feel this is a dangerous assumption. Perhaps in some instances there is no doubt on either side and this final session is indeed a mere formality, but for most this will be the first time the candidating pastor will meet with the congregation as a whole, and both parties will need this time to really make up their minds about the situation. Neither side ought to be pressured into feeling the decision has to be made before the candidate comes for the final meeting. I suppose that notion stems from the financial expense usually involved in bringing a candidate in.

In fact, I would go so far as to suggest the church not take its vote immediately after the final meeting, if it is determined the congregation needs some time to let things "soak in" and pray about their decision. Choosing a pastor is an awesome task and responsibility, and I shudder to think how often it is rushed into. The pastor and family may also need time to arrive at their decision concerning the call. Candidating is an intense, emotionally-draining experience and sometimes one gains a little perspective when finally removed from the situation.

We were positive that after we visited this church in Vermont if they called me we would *know* this was where God was leading. When they did call me, we fortunately had already decided we would not give them our decision that day because as it turned out, we were still undecided. We both desperately wanted to do the Lord's will and we were so afraid we might choose that which was not His plan. We were willing to stay in our present pastorate despite the frustration we were feeling, if that was, indeed, where God wanted us. On the other hand, we were ready to strike out into new and unexpected territory if He so willed.

The agonizing feeling of doubt in the pit of our stomachs was growing daily—what if we picked to move and God really wanted us to stay? Conversely, what if we resolved to remain and God was offering us this new opportunity on a silver platter? After all, hadn't we been in the right place at the right time for the right phone call? More than once we considered putting out various fleeces to ascertain God's will but felt such action would only serve to prove a lack of faith on our part.

On the way home from our final candidating time, we visited again with our pastor friend in whose kitchen this whole dilemma had begun. We both highly valued his counsel and decided to ask him what he thought we should do and then go along with his decision. He refused to make the decision for us.

We asked him why God didn't write His answer in the sky instead of frustrating us so. We shared our desperate fears about making a decision that would be out of the will of God. It was at that point that our dear friend, with many more years in the ministry than I, gave me some wonderful wisdom which has since seen me through many more difficult decisions. "You shouldn't think that the will of God is always singular," he said. "Maybe it could be God's will for you to be in either place."

I had never thought of that. I had been so hung up on the fact that one of these churches must be the right church and the other one the wrong church, I hadn't even considered the notion that perhaps God could use me in either place. There certainly was nothing in either situation that I could see would biblically prohibit me from being pastor in it, so perhaps the decision was indeed up to me and I could trust God to use me to glorify Him in either place. What a relief! There wasn't just one single church in the whole wide world—that I had to somehow find—where God wanted me to be pastor. Perhaps there were dozens or more which I could pastor and God would bless my efforts.

Gordon MacDonald, pastor and counselor, expressed the same idea in his book *Magnificent Marriage* when he addresses the subject of finding *the* right partner:

> I have never been convinced that the will of God has involved his selection of one specific person for each of us to marry. I remember how many times this kind of logic was foisted upon us when we were young. Somewhere out there . . . is a lovely girl the Lord has picked out for you, I was told . . . If we seriously believe there

is only "one best" person in the world for us, what happens if the "one best" makes a bad decision somewhere on the trail to our special meeting . . . I am of the settled opinion now that each of us could probably have married any one of a number of different persons and been happy.[1]

I, too, am of the same opinion concerning that "one best" church out there "somewhere."

In all honesty, my wife and I wouldn't have minded some handwriting in the sky telling us this was the "one best" church, but at least the terror of making a fatal mistake was gone. We prayed some more, and we talked some more. We called them back and turned down the call.

For the first time since the turmoil began, both my wife and I felt the peace of God. We knew in our hearts we had—for us—made the right decision. God honored that decision, and very soon afterwards we began to see much fruit in the church. Even now as we look back, we are so thankful we made the decision to "stick it out."

So, why did this phone call and chain of events even come about? I don't really know for sure. Without a doubt it was a turning point in my ministry in my first church. After I made the decision to remain, the Spirit began to move in the church and in me in a fresh way. I know I learned a great deal about discerning the will of God as I struggled to separate fleshly desires from His heavenly plans. I also discovered the first of several styles that pulpit committees and churches have for interviewing a prospective pastor.

This Vermont church had what I've come to identify as

"The Marathon Weekend." This is the interviewing technique where so many meetings with so many different committees and boards are scheduled—not to mention all the various eating opportunities—that the candidating pastor feels as if he has just run a marathon. To run this type of marathon, one needs to be able, in the span of 48 hours, to meet with the entire church and answer questions, have dinner with at least three key families and answer questions, meet with the men's group and answer questions, meet at least twice with the pulpit committee and answer questions, meet with the youth group and answer questions, meet with all the board chairpersons and answer questions, and finally have a congregational dinner and—guess what—answer questions! Should one survive, he may very well be the person for this church. However, when returning home after such a weekend and the candidate's wife asks what he wants for dinner— another question—he will predictably go into cardiac arrest and require CPR!

Now the opposite of "The Marathon Weekend" is what I call the "It's Your Move" pulpit committee. This is the one where you walk in the door, shake hands all around, sit down and the chairperson turns to you and says, "Now, what do you want to do?"

I first experienced this awkward situation when searching for my first pastorate. The chairman was very friendly and gracious—he simply had no planned agenda or questions for me. I was supposed to conduct the entire interview. No one on the committee seemed prepared with any questions or ideas either. I was amazed at how little thought had been given to the selection of the person God was calling to be their pastor. Actually, it was indicative of the entire church situation; they were, as Scripture describes, a people without a vision (see Prov. 29:18).

After fidgeting through this so-called interview, I welcomed the idea of a pulpit committee who had done it's homework and had questions and concerns dropping from everyone's lips. Little did I know that this approach can also be taken to an extreme and what results is what I term "The Inquisition."

Some may be curious as to what goes on in a pastor's mind when facing a candidating experience. While I obviously cannot speak for all pastors, the time with Old Second Church remains forever etched in my mind. I had an easier time at my ordination council. I am tempted to say Tituba, the accused slave, had an easier time at the Salem Witch Trials. No doubt Rudolph Hess had it easier at Nuremberg.

It all began with what felt like the condemned's last meal: an expensive restaurant with a tremendous menu. There I sat with the committee and leaders of the church, anxiously awaiting to see in what price range they ordered. My appetite had long since nervously disappeared as I fielded question upon question about me and my ministry. All I could think was "what a way to ruin a good meal." How much I would have liked to be alone with my wife and daughter for a quiet dinner and prayerful preparation for the real encounter to come.

That was when I met for a time of "sharing" with the whole church. There we sat in the fellowship hall with my back against the wall—in more ways than one!—and with the congregation in a semi-circle, like hungry wolves around me. Then the barrage began—question upon question. It seemed to go on for hours. Now, don't misunderstand; there were many good and honest questions asked by sincere and concerned people. There were just so many of them! My brain began to feel like mush and I was glad I had eaten lightly.

Sandwiched between the sincere inquiries were others which seemed loaded and full of barbs. Several people were bringing up topics which I garnered were their personal pet peeves. I was getting a glimpse of what Jesus must have felt like when the Pharisees were constantly trying to trip Him up on points of the Law.

One recently divorced man, with an angry look in his eyes, asked if I would allow a divorced person to be on the church board. Another man asked me where I thought our denomination "was at." I had the feeling he was anti-denomination and wanted me to pin a label on it like "too liberal" or "hopeless." I also had the sense that no matter how I answered it would be wrong. I escaped by making it a joke and telling him where our denominational headquarters was located. Thank goodness, he laughed too.

Again, don't get me wrong. I don't believe this group of people deliberately set out to question me to death. From their perspective they probably wanted to find out everything about me so they could be sure when they voted on my call. However, from my vantage point, it was emotionally draining. To top it all off, I was supposed to get a good night's rest afterwards in a hot motel room with a pregnant wife and a year-and-a-half old child in tow! I hardly felt prepared to preach with power and relevancy the next morning. But there was no turning back now and I preached the next morning and the congregation voted the next week.

Against better judgment, I put out the proverbial fleece. I asked God if He wanted me to go there that the call would be unanimous. I requested this in spite of the fact the committee warned me there was one person who always voted against everyone and everything.

My reception from the congregation and committee after my sermon was overwhelmingly positive. I began to have some good feelings about the whole "ordeal." In a few days the chairman called me with the vote. He was pleased about it; I was not. There were two votes against me—one being the perennial negative voter, he said. The fleece was barely damp. I reluctantly turned down the call.

The shocking end to this story is that I later accepted a second call to the same church. As time went on, I became more restless in my present situation and kept pondering "if only I hadn't turned down Old Second Church" and berating myself for insisting upon a unanimous vote.

Finally, after seven months, I could stand it no longer. I became convinced the grass was most assuredly greener on the other side and I had turned it down. I threw out just a tiny fleece and called the pulpit committee chairman at Old Second Church just to "see how things were going." To my surprise and pleasure, he said he had been thinking a great deal about me lately—that inevitable "coincidence" again! The committee had searched through dozens of profiles of potential pastors but still kept coming back to mine. Now the tiny fleece was really getting damp.

I agreed to have my name placed back before the committee and soon afterwards they unanimously voted to have me come back and candidate again. I really would have liked a unanimous vote from the congregation this time but remembered what happened before when I "almost" got it and decided against making this a criterion for my acceptance. No inquisition this time; just a sermon and a vote. It was two against, just as before, except that this time it was two different people. Mr. Negative hadn't shown up for this vote!

As I look back now I can't completely recall why I

decided to accept that second call. Deep inside, I had misgivings about it. Everything on the surface seemed biblically fine and there were many things about the new situation which looked good to me: it was located in a part of the country where we wanted to live; it was a smaller, but seemingly more mature group of Christians than our present church; and there was the realistic possibility of further schooling which I wanted to pursue. Still, a small voice inside me seemed to say something was wrong.

I realize our feelings are fallen because of sin and they can't always be a reliable indicator of the truth in every situation, but there is something I call "sanctified common sense" which is usually a pretty good barometer. Sometimes just plain old common sense is all you need to know something's not right.

I remember when we candidated at a small New England church and the pulpit committee chairman's wife who was entertaining us turned to my wife and asked her: "And how old are you, dear?" When my wife told her age, the woman smugly turned to her husband with, "I told you she was just a baby!" It didn't take the wisdom of Solomon to see there were going to be problems of acceptance here!

But in other situations the facts are not so clear-cut and logic is often muddled. Sanctified common sense is listening to those inner feelings which are prompted by the Holy Spirit. How I wish I had listened a little more to my heart and a little less to my head when I made that fateful decision to accept the second call to Old Second Church.

I call it a "fateful" decision because there has not been such a mismatch since David and Goliath. I'm sure Moses had an easier time in the wilderness getting the grumbling Israelites to follow him than I had in getting these people to follow me in my short tenure there as pastor. The leaders of the church and I were on entirely different wavelengths as far as goals and objectives for ministry were concerned. In fact I learned just prior to my leaving the church that when they initially called me it was not without some apprehension on their part as well. But they chose me anyway with the thought they could *change* me when I got there.

I know unequivocally this is no way to start a marriage—man to woman or church to pastor. In fact, in my premarital counseling sessions I usually ask a couple, "How are you planning to change one another?" Certainly, changes come both in a pastor's life and in a church's, but to start a relationship with the presumed strategy for change will only lead to problems between husband and wife or church and pastor. There must be a good "marriage" of compatibility or all concerned are headed for trouble. This lack of compatibility or a similar philosophy of ministry is not always easy to discern. At other times, red flags go up in a way that can't be mistaken.

I remember meeting with a pulpit committee in a fashionable suburb of a large city. As we talked it became apparent we had very divergent views as to the authority of Scripture. Although it would have been a challenge to work in that situation, it would also have been a battle. They recognized this and sent me a very nice letter explaining the importance of compatibility between pastor and church. Needless to say, we were not. No fleeces needed here!

I sometimes still agonize over how I could have been so wrong about Old Second Church. I had spent a great deal of time beforehand corresponding, as well as meeting, with people in the church. I had sent questionnaires to the pulpit committee and congregation at large to help get a grass roots feeling for the church. Still, what I expected to find when I got there—a church of mature believers anxiously awaiting a shepherd to lead them into vibrant and exciting ministry—was not what awaited me. Instead, I found a church with years of dissension and many critical spirits which direly needed a doctor to bring about some healing. How could I have completely missed this in all the hours I spent with the committee and church?

As I think back over the situation and many others I have since encountered in my candidating experiences, I am convinced the view a candidate gets of the church—and probably the church of a candidate—is very one-sided. The church puts its best foot forward and usually *only* its best foot. Skeletons are shoved in the closet and not brought out at least until the pastor has unpacked and the moving van has pulled away!

Likewise, the candidating pastor dwells on personal strengths, accomplishments and areas of giftedness while failing to mention weaknesses and areas of needed growth.

The picture this committee had given me of its church was a very inacccurate one. It may have been how they thought they were, or even how they wished to be; but it was not the way they presently were. I have since decided it is truly a giant leap of faith when one accepts a call to a church because it is nigh impossible to obtain a true picture of the entire congregation. A candidate's knowledge of the church is filtered through a small, select group and often it is not a truly representative one. Old Second Church had a large group of elderly parishioners who felt cut off from the decision makers of the church and not one of them was on the pulpit committee.

One other factor I regrettably neglected when making my decision about accepting the call at Old Second was my wife's feelings on the matter. I believe when the candidating pastor hears God's voice calling that the spouse should hear it, too. I feel this strongly even if the spouse works outside the home and is not as involved with the ministry as the traditional pastor's wife. Pastor and spouse should be agreed that indeed God is calling them to this particular church.

This was not exactly the case when I accepted the second call. My wife, who is very involved with me in ministry, expressed some doubts and fears about my abilities to relate well with the inner circle of leaders at Old Second. She went on to share what she was afraid might happen if we went there. I dismissed these fears lightly. Seeing how frustrated I was in our present church and being afraid she was keeping me from something I really wanted, she began to support me in my desire to go to Old Second and even agreed with me to accept the final call there, despite her misgivings.

During the two years we were at the church she never said "I told you so!" but she might well have. It had happened almost exactly as she feared. I should have known that my life partner ought to be the one who knew me best. I should have listened more intently to her caring instincts. She, of all people, knew my strengths and weaknesses and felt from the beginning that this new "marriage" might be a mismatch. Candidating pastors ought to appreciate their spouse's insights and not reject them lightly, as I did. I firmly believe that when God calls, He calls both husband and wife, and there is something amiss if both partners are not hearing the same clear call.

As I reminisce over the churches at which I've candidated (for awhile I felt like a "professional candidate" as in each new situation I strove to do everything right *this* time), I am now more at peace about knowing when the Lord is calling. I recently heard a pastor sum up his decision-making process, and his methods are definitely akin to mine.

Given that the prospective church is theologically, and for the most part, similar in philosophy of ministry to the candidate, my friend asks the question: "Will my gifts and abilities be such that I can help them where they are in their ministry?" If the answer is affirmative, he sees this as a pull to the new church. If this pull corresponds to a desire to move on—or a push—from the present situation, he then adds that it is a good possibility the Lord is calling. With all these factors present, I would venture to say the fleece would definitely be more than damp!

How Do *You* Identify?

Who among us has never felt like Gideon? A decision must be made and yet we find that we cannot choose, for we are not sure what God's will is for us in this particular matter. If only God would give us a clear sign, an unmistakable indication as to what to do, which way to go, what direction to take.

Pastors and parishioners alike struggle daily with God's will for their lives. For some, the struggle is more painful and intense as the issues grow in importance. How wonderful it would be if only we could discover a fool-proof formula for determining God's perfect will in every instance. Life would be so much easier. But would it be better?

When we were younger, more immature, it seemed as if life was simpler. Other people made decisions for us. So much of what we did then was dictated by the decisions of our parents and guardians. But as we grew and matured, more of the responsibility for making decisions fell into our own hands.

So it is with our relationship with the Lord. To a certain extent, many decisions have already been made for us by virtue of the fact that we have become followers of Jesus Christ. His Lordship over us brings with it certain requirements, certain responsibilities. The picture begins to lose focus, however, as we struggle to determine just how we will choose to carry out His perfect will for our lives.

For example, it is God's will that we worship Him, but it is our choice as to where we will worship. It is God's will that we read and study His Word, but it is up to each one of us to choose the chapter and verse. It is God's will that we serve Him according to our gifts, but it is up to us to decide in which way or form that service is to take place. God's perfect will for our lives may take us down any one of many roads; it is our choice to embark on the journey. How much easier it would be, if only God would give us a road map marked in red!

And how much easier it would be if God were to mark the right pastor for the right church in red (or put a big red X on the church's steeple). It would certainly take all of the guesswork (and prayerful thought and consideration) out of candidating for all concerned. But then, how much value would there be to such a process if each church and candidate came so clearly marked? Just as we grew and matured through the decision-making process in our personal lives, so we must grow in our spiritual and corporate lives and relationships, as we struggle to make important decisions as the Body of Christ.

The decision to call a pastor or choose a church may not ever be easy, but we can make the process more comfortable. Candidating is a stressful situation for all involved. It can be a rewarding, exciting, maturing experience, but the responsibility placed on each member of the committee to choose the "perfect pastor" can carry with it a great deal of tension. Marathon candidating weekends do little to relieve that tension. It would be wiser to spend more sessions with fewer candidates than several marathon sessions to determine which of 65 candidates might be "God's will" for the church.

Next, it is important that since both the church and new pastor are making a commitment to one another, honesty at the outset is a must. Both should be up front with not only strengths and weaknesses, but with expectations as well. Candidating sessions should allow both parties to share needs and to be able to talk about personal matters in an atmosphere of trust.

And finally, what do you do when the fleece is just barely damp? As a pastor, you have been struggling with the choice of more than one new opportunity for ministry. As a pulpit committee, you have narrowed down the choice to at least three "perfect" candidates for the job. As a pastor you could serve the Lord effectively in either church. As a member of the pulpit committee, you believe that any one of the candidates could meet the needs of the congregation. Is there a clear-cut answer? If so, that would be making the decision for you. You must decide for yourself. And as you learn to live with that decision, you will grow even more into the will of God.

4

"I've Fallen In Love with Someone Else"

He had counseled many who were feeling the pains of divorce. Now it was he—the pastor— who needed the consoling. His wife of eight years wanted a divorce. What would his congregation think? How would his deacons react? Would he ever recover from hearing his wife say, "I'm going to divorce you"?

"I'm not sure how to tell you this, but I'm going to divorce you. For some time I haven't loved you. I've fallen in love with someone else."

With those words, 30 years of my living a quiet, generally unspectacular life were shattered. The date was Friday, October 17, 1980. The memories of that night—the look in her eyes, the horrible feeling of being involved in a tragedy happening in slow motion—will be with me for the rest of my life.

Three years prior to that night we had moved to our new home and begun life among our new church family with the eager anticipation and excitement that comes with a new pastorate. The church family had done much to make us feel at home, and soon friendships began to form as we fit ourselves into the pace of the community.

Our son was two years old at the time of our move and he received more than his share of attention. Many of the leaders of the church took it upon themselves to make up for his lack of local grandparents.

A year and a half later, a beautiful daughter arrived at the parsonage. We were thrilled with this new addition to our family. The pregnancy and delivery went well, and soon we were enjoying all the sleepless nights and diaper changes that go with a newborn!

On that infamous Friday, October 17, the pastors and wives of several surrounding churches were scheduled to get together for their monthly supper and time of fellowship. A different parsonage family hosted the event each month and that time it was held in a neighboring town 15 minutes from where we lived. The gathering was uneventful and, as we left and were walking to the car, I said to Maxine, "Let's go for a ride so we can talk a little longer."

The years have blurred many of the details, but I remember sensing a strange uneasiness as we walked to the car. As we headed in a roundabout way for home, I said, "I want to talk to you about some odd feelings I've been having. Is there something we need to talk about; is there anything wrong?"

My wife replied, "Let's go home and talk." We drove the next five miles in silence. As I took the baby-sitter home, it felt as if there was a lightning storm going on inside my stomach. To this day I've never experienced anything quite like it. It was a kind of awful dread about what was going to take place. I wonder if it would be the same feeling you would get if you heard on the radio that a nuclear bomb would drop on your area in five minutes; I don't know. But I knew that I was about to hear something from my wife that would shake my world.

The house was silent as I walked in. The two children were asleep upstairs, totally oblivious to the change that was about to take place in their lives. Maxine asked me to sit down—not next to her, but on another sofa, one placed 90 degrees from where she was sitting.

In carefully chosen, calm words she said, "I had wanted to wait until Sunday night, after you were finished with your preaching, before I told you. But since you have raised the question, I'll tell you now."

She wanted a divorce. The love was gone. There was another person.

Our eight years of marriage were over. I was in emotional shock; I couldn't cry. I had heard news like this in the privacy of my office, and I always tried to remain objective while the other person experienced the wide range of emotions that go with life's crises.

I sat there not feeling a thing. And I began to ask questions. "What are your plans? What about the kids? Have you been thinking about this for a long time? Is there any possibility that we could get some counseling and work this out?"

The answer to the last question was never to change. No.

On that night when the life we'd experienced as man and wife was crumbling down, God in His mercy spared me the full impact of what was being said. I didn't feel the sharp pain of a dagger reaching its mark. I felt numbness—the kind you might experience when given a spinal for anesthesia. You know the operation is going on, you hear the scalpels and needles doing their work, but you don't feel a thing.

Rev. Howard Roberts was and still is one of my closest friends. I called him at 11:30 p.m. and gave him the grim details. I needed help. I got in the car and began the 20-mile drive to his house. Upon leaving town there is a bridge with concrete supports. For the first time in my life I considered suicide. For one fleeting moment I considered that it might be a way of escape from the trap I was suddenly in.

Just as quickly as the thought came, I can see now that God filled my head with all of the many things I had to live for. Friends, like Howard, who cared for me; a career as a pastor; two wonderful children, who were just getting old enough to relate to as people; parents who loved me deeply and fully supported my work; a brother and sister who cared for me. Since that brief moment, the consideration of ending life intentionally has never been an option, but I'll always remember the moment when those thoughts were a reality. It has been a point of identification with others who struggle with suicide for long periods of time. I can't say I thank God for that moment of crisis, but like so many of the difficulties we go and grow through, God used it.

Howard was groggy with sleep but very gracious when I arrived. He had the coffee ready and we sat in his office for a couple of hours. I just needed a caring person to be present while the reality of what was happening set in. Howard listened lovingly. To this day, the bond between us is stronger because of that horrible night we spent together. Someone has said, "A friend in need is a friend indeed." Howard was one of several friends whom God used as human crutches to carry a broken pastor.

As I drove over the bridge on the way home, I thanked God for His intervention on my behalf. That bridge is a shrine to the goodness of God to me.

When I got home it was evident that the cat and I were to share the living room couch from now on. The blankets, sheets and pillows were placed on a chair in the living room. Quietly, I went upstairs and stood beside my two kids' beds. The sounds of their breathing have always been a joy to listen to, but on this night they seemed more precious than ever. As I stood over their beds a heaviness hung over me like the chains of the Ghost of Christmas Past in Dickens' *A Christmas Carol.* What would become of them? Would I share the privilege of being with them as they grew up? Would they live with me? Would they still call me Dad?

The sun was scheduled to come up in a few hours. Saturday was going to be a busy day. A trip to a meeting could be cancelled, but the final preparations for Sunday still had to be made. The cat and I settled down to get some rest. I know from personal observation the cat got three hours of uninterrupted sleep.

At this point, only four people knew what was going on. I needed to break the news to my deacons as soon as possible, but my first priority was to make it through Sunday. Our family went through the motions of a "normal" Saturday. The kids kept busy doing whatever two young kids do on a rainy, cold fall afternoon. Their parents just existed. I kept wanting time to go by faster yet did not have anything to look forward to. Another night came, a second night with no sleep.

I've never liked going to church alone. It just doesn't

seem right leaving the family at home and silently riding to the church building. To the questions about the missing pastor's wife I truthfully replied, "She just wasn't able to come today and the kids stayed home with her."

There I was, standing in front of 160 people. My insides were aching. I was exhausted from lack of sleep. And worst of all, I couldn't share what I was going through. Not yet. Not until Tuesday evening when the deacons would come to the parsonage and meet with me. I praise God for giving me the strength to make it through my most difficult Sunday ever, October 19, 1980.

I asked Howard if he would please attend my meeting with the deacons. Immediately after the kids were put to bed, my wife left for the evening. I had no idea what to expect. My purpose was to give these church leaders all the facts and together decide on the next move. Several of the men began to cry. There was silence. One by one these brothers in Christ got up and gave me a hug without saying a word. They listened while I presented what they needed to hear. With Howard present, both for moral support and as an objective third party, we began to make plans for the immediate future.

I have always taken seriously the role of the Church as the Body of Christ. If the Body is to function in a healthy way, there needs to be the ability of its members to share life's experiences with each other. This includes both the joyful and the painful. I told the deacons that I needed to model that kind of openness in my present crisis. Instead of having someone else fill the pulpit and read a letter, instead of suddenly disappearing for a couple of weeks, I felt a need to be with my church family. I needed to let them minister to me, as I hurt.

I don't presume to say that other people's ways of handling this situation have been wrong. I just know that this was the correct way for me to handle my circumstance.

With the encouragement of the deacons, I began to prepare for the next Sunday. I wanted even my tragic news to be used in ways that would honor God. I prayed for His wisdom. I believe He answered.

The title—"No Greater Strength"; the text— Philippians 4:13, "I can do everything through him who gives me strength."

This history of God's relationship with man is lined with people discovering the limits of personal strength and literally having to depend upon God's strength alone to carry on. I could speak of Noah who found strength to build the ark, in spite of public criticism. We could consider Abraham who was asked to sacrifice his son Isaac on Mount Moriah. I could remind you of David who found strength in his time of mourning for his lost son.

But today the example is more personal than that of these men of the Bible. Today, in a very open way, I want to testify to the strength God has offered me. A week ago Friday night, I was told that my wife has not loved me for some time and that her affections have recently been turned to another person. She has filed for a divorce and plans to remarry as soon as possible.

I am endeavoring, as your pastor, to act as a Christian man during this time. I am trying to show Christian love to my wife. I am willing and eager to work towards a reconciliation. I have asked God's and Maxine's forgiveness for my responsibility in the failure of our marriage.

It is only because of my honest attempts to live up to these responsibilities that I am able to face you this morning with a sense of dignity and to greet you at the conclusion of the service.

If you see Maxine, please show Christian love to her, for she needs it in a special way.

To those of you who are married, in no way should this be a sign of approval of divorce, but rather an object lesson to you on the horror of this tragic decision. Whenever God's plan is broken, the consequences are painful and long lasting. Let this be a time for you to gird up your marriage.

Friends, this is a time when our Christianity will be tested in full public view. Nonbelievers will try to get mileage out of this, but if you and I together simply follow the guidelines in God's Word, this could be a mighty witness for our community. God hasn't been given a black eye, but a chance to show His great love and faithfulness.

Our church hasn't been dealt a fatal blow, but has been given an opportunity to be a beacon of Christian love and compassion in a world that desperately needs those qualities. Together we can show our community that it does make a difference to have Jesus Christ as Lord of our lives.

I covet your prayers for my family during our time of need. I also pledge to make you proud of my conduct during the coming months.

In the words of Paul, "We are hard pressed on every side, but not crushed; perplexed, but not in despair; persecuted, but not abandoned; struck down, but not destroyed. We always carry around in our body the death of Jesus, so that the life of Jesus may also be revealed in our body" (2 Cor. 4:8-10).

I thank God for your love and for His strength which is from everlasting to everlasting.

One by one, the congregation came out the door. Some were crying, some completely silent, some with just a word or two accompanied by a firm handshake. Some said later that they were just too hurt to face me. These kind, loving people had taken a young pastor who had just made himself very vulnerable and began to love him back to life!

While my wife went away for several weeks, my parents came to watch over the children and provide some moral support. They had received the news as if someone had told them about the death of one of their children. Divorce had always been something horrible that happened to other families. It was never talked about in terms of happening to anyone in our immediate family. In their quiet, caring way, they were there when I needed them. For two weeks, we comforted each other. The children enjoyed Grandma's good home cooking and Dad busied himself with minor repairs around the house.

While my parents visited, I began to have counseling sessions with a neighboring pastor, Dr. Gary Johnson. Not only do Gary and I have a close friendship, but I value him as a good listener and sounding board. Gary is blessed with an ability to help others focus their thinking and offer sound guidance and direction. During the three or four sessions we had together, I talked and he listened most of the time. The question, "Why?" kept coming up over and over. After a while I could see the futility of asking what could have been done differently, and I began to consider the future.

I had to decide what I was going to do regarding my job; what about the kids; what legal help I would need; what financial arrangements had to be made? With all these issues needing attention, the paralyzing numbness soon gave way to the harsh cold facts of reality. I needed someone to listen, as I tried to bring structure out of chaos.

I had never been in an attorney's office before. For awhile it was to become my second home. I could have bought a paperback book that advertises a "Do-It-Yourself Divorce." They may work for some, but it was great comfort to be able to direct my thousands of questions to another human being.

I was completely ignorant of all that a divorce involves. Each state has its own set of laws, and even though laws change on a regular basis, I found that in our state it's possible to get a divorce on the grounds of "incompatibility." That is a fancy word for not getting along. If one person wants out of the marriage, that's it. There's very little the other partner can do to stop the process. Once the clock starts ticking towards the court date, it's just a matter of time before the judge simply grants the divorce. Maxine's petition would be granted and there was nothing I could do to stop it.

The waiting period covered the months of November

and December. In a normal year those are hectic times, but this year they were almost impossible. The kids looked forward to Thanksgiving and Christmas with excitement and happiness. God seemed to be sparing these two precious children the tremendous pain their parents were going through.

I cooked the Thanksgiving turkey, and the two children and I invited another church family in for dinner. Thank God for friends. Several families from the church shared our dinner and for a few brief hours, the constant pain seemed to fade into the background.

Only a few Christmas cards were sent out that year, and as Christmas shopping was perfunctorily done, the presents were deposited at the post office. For the last time, our family gathered around the tree and exchanged presents with each other. In 12 days we would no longer be husband and wife, but for now exchanged one last gift. My gift was a slowcooker; it sits unused to this day in the place I set it five years ago.

The new year came. The divorce became final. I was single again. Lord, help me!

If I'd had time to panic, I probably would have. But for the next three and a half months, I was a single father. I'd get up at 6:15 to get myself ready and then get the kids up at 6:45. My five-year-old son could just about get himself half ready, but my 18-month-old daughter needed considerable help. How those kids survived mismatched clothes, unusual meals and baths that only a father can give, I'll never know. But we made it. It was especially fun when I had a 7:00 A.M. meeting and had to get the kids to the baby-sitter by 6:45.

Our baby-sitter, Claudie, was a lifesaver. She and her family rescued us more times than I care to remember.

Many nights she and other church families would have a hot meal waiting for us. There was never a moment when Claudie made us feel anything less than a part of her own family. She was another person God used to minister to me during my ordeal.

In April, another part of my life was torn away. In a preliminary hearing, the judge ruled in my ex-wife's favor regarding the custody of our two children. This decision was made permanent later in the summer. On that awful April afternoon, as the kids watched, I packed all their clothes into several large plastic bags and gave both kids and clothes over to my ex-wife. That was the last time my kids and I lived permanently together under the same roof.

In the midst of these hectic months of being a single parent, pastoring a church, consulting with the lawyer and generally keeping my head above water, I was also the executive chairman of the John Wesley White Crusade of Northern Maine and Western New Brunswick. It was my privilege to work with an outstanding group of local leaders and a godly group of men from the Billy Graham Evangelistic Association.

When I first learned about the upcoming divorce, I presented the facts of the situation to our crusade executive committee. It was important for me to not create a stumbling block for any of the crusade activities. Things had been going very well and I didn't want my personal situation to be a tool Satan would use against our united crusade effort. In their wisdom the executive committee expressed complete support and I continued my job until our committee disbanded after the crusade.

With the clarity that comes from the perspective of time I can see how God used the crusade and its related activities as a custom-made spiritual life jacket for me. I was too busy to worry over my situation. I was ministered to by an assortment of team members that had a gracious sensitivity to my life struggles. They provided listening ears and wise counsel at a time when it was needed.

I am convinced that God used Howard Roberts, Gary Johnson, these crusade team members and other close pastoral friends to help me realize that I still had something to offer the Kingdom of God. In the midst of my life being torn into pieces, their godly wisdom was instrumental in my coming out of the experience a healthy, useful person, one who could remain in the ministry. I shall always be grateful to God for those "angels" whom He sent my way.

God's providential care never fails to amaze me. He has things so perfectly timed. The very April week when I was in court listening as the lawyers argued over who should have custody of our children was also the week I was on the crusade platform with Dr. White. The clear presentation of the gospel, though very familiar, served as a daily reminder of God's faithfulness even to a pastor with a broken heart.

The natives say we have only two seasons—11 months of winter and one month of rough sledding. Summer finally did arrive in 1981, and it brought with it a refreshing change of pace and a time of relaxation. My annual visit to my childhood home took on new meaning as my two children and I spent several weeks together with my family.

That summer, the kids and I began building a new type of bond that continues to this day. We began to get into a routine of visiting each other every other weekend. Every four days they have come to expect a phone call from me at 6:00 P.M. Now that my daughter is old enough to carry on a conversation, she's making up for all the times I had to carry on a one-sided conversation. It is a beautiful thing to pray with my kids over the phone. By my example, I want them to realize that prayer is an important part of their daily lives. We pray for everything, from a Little League game to a pet's injury. Through the years they are learning that prayer is a normal part of life. Thank God for telephones!

It would be impossible for me to overestimate the love and support of my church family. Through the entire ordeal they supported me and held me up in prayer. From the beginning I chose to be open with them on what was taking place. Through the use of several "fireside chats" after the morning services, I kept them up-to-date on what was happening. I wanted them to get the facts from me, rather than hear them at the local coffee shop! I was also careful not to continually discuss this event in sermons and other public presentations. When it was natural for the topic to come up, fine. But I didn't want my personal life to be continually on the front burner of everyone's mind. We had many other, more useful, things to be doing.

I can appreciate how difficult my presence was for some in the congregation. "That guy up there behind our pulpit has been divorced!" I could almost hear them say. With only a rare exception, those few in the congregation who were troubled, graciously waited upon the Lord for Him to work things out.

I, too, laid my service as pastor of that church before the Lord. Taking things day by day, I was willing to obey God in whatever He directed. Writing this five years later, He still has not directed me to move elsewhere.

And now, after patiently waiting on the Lord to put my

life back together, I can tell you that God brought someone else into my life. Carolyn had been saved in our church and was much loved by the church family. God sent me someone who had the right spiritual gifts to love a hurting, but healing man, and to love two young children as her very own. Dr. Gary Johnson performed the wedding ceremony which included much worship and praise to a loving and faithful God. God had lead me full circle, from the bleak hopelessness to the joyful expectancy of a new marriage.

There are those who take exception to remarriage under any circumstances, but I thank God the people among whom I am privileged to minister understand the grace of God, His mercy and compassion, and the need for them to extend this to the divorced in their midst.

God has an amazing way of blunting the memory of pain that occurs during the tragedies of life. That is one of His many gifts to us. For me, the facts of the divorce and its aftermath have faded. The intense pain and emptiness I felt are gone. There are some lingering scars that remain that we, as divorced individuals, carry with us through life, but even those will fade in time.

There are times when I go into one of the kids' bedrooms when they are not there, and have to leave the room. Sometimes when the neighborhood kids are swinging in our backyard, flashes of two other kids swinging come to mind. We love to share our yard with our friends, but sometimes I ask, "Lord, why? Why couldn't there be two more kids playing and running out back?" I've learned that it's no use fighting the misty eyes when I see a play or movie that involves children in tender situations. Inside, my heart aches for something I know I can't have at the present time.

Even writing this narrative has been painful, but it has

been a real time of therapy for me. This has been the first time I've relived the entire sequence of events at one sitting. Through this experience I've been reminded once again just how completely God kept His hand on me. In bringing just the right people into my life, He provided perfect pastoral care for a broken pastor. As long as I live I shall be an example of His ability to sustain and support.

To you who are reading this and who can identify with what I've written, may God be with you. My prayer for you is that you will understand that even though at times it seems that there is little to live for, God will reward a repentant, obedient heart. Hang on to Him. Think of the story you've just read and let God do a wonderful work in your life.

"I can do everything through him who gives me strength" (Phil. 4:13).

How Do *You* Identify?

Whatever happened to those words of the apostle Paul, "And now these three remain: faith, hope and love. But the greatest of these is love" (1 Cor. 13:13). If love is really so powerful, if it is able to endure so many things, if, according to Paul, it never fails, then why does it?

That is a question that more than one-half of all married couples in the United States have to deal with for this is the number of marriages that will end in divorce. Nonbelievers seem to have no difficulty falling in and out of love. But it's different for believers, for those who have a relationship firmly rooted in a common faith and commitment to the Lordship of Jesus Christ. Isn't it?

The shocking fact is that more and more Christian marriages are ending in divorce. More and more believers are saying to their spouses, "I've fallen in love with someone else." It happens to people in our prayer fellowships. It happens to parents of the young people in our youth groups. It happens to those serving on various church boards. It even happens to pastors.

In the reality of this ever-growing situation, we need to ask, how do we as members of the Body of Christ react to those in ministry and to those in the pew who are hurting because someone they deeply love has just walked out of their life, and divorce is just around the corner?

First, we note that people become divorced from one another, not necessarily from the Body. And yet, the effect is often one and the same. Over 40 years ago, when a young woman heard the devastating words from her spouse, she was eventually left with three children, no husband and no church, for shortly after she was divorced from her husband, the church divorced her from its membership list.

That was 40 years ago, but it seems some believers would like to continue that trend today. It may be a result of our own personal theology or it may be that deep down, some pastors and lay persons see the divorce of one of their own members as a failure on the part of the church, that it was not successful in its nurturing or teaching and as a result, a marriage failed. To divorce the remaining member of a marriage from our church roll or from church fellowship makes it easier for the rest to deal with what they perceive as their own shortcoming. But what does such an attitude on our part really accomplish? We only say to that hurting member that we, too, have no love to share with them.

We should also note the therapeutic value of membership within a loving and caring Christian community. To
lose the love of a spouse is painful and it may be that only
time will eventually heal that pain. But the love and care of
a surrounding church family can also do much to make life
more bearable in the meantime. Just as we surround a
grieving member of our church who has lost a spouse due
to death, we should also surround and care for the one
who has lost a spouse due to divorce. Each of us can play a
part in this therapy. Our words of compassion and understanding may be a beginning, but often are not enough.
Don't just speak, act. Acts of love and kindness, like an
apple pie or casserole or offer to baby-sit, really add much
more to the healing touch. Both words and acts say we
care and love.

In addition, the healing process might be more effective if we also temper our own personal theology and doc-
trines concerning divorce and remarriage with a bit of
patience. Jesus does have something to say about the lasting nature of marriage (see Mark 10:1-10) and divorce
(see Matthew 5:31,32), and the apostle Paul certainly has
some strong viewpoints on both (see 1 Cor. 7). Your
church may have its own doctrine, conservative or liberal,
concerning divorced members and remarriage. But one
week after a church member's marriage has broken up is
not the proper time to elaborate on church doctrine.

No one who is hurting, grieving or struggling with the
pain of losing someone they might still be very much in
love with, needs the extra burden of our personal or doctrinal theology, no matter how gently we try to share it.
What they do need is our care, our love and our deepest
understanding.

5

The Great Slam Dunk!
And Other Stories

What would you do if you went to pick up your paycheck and in its place received shopping bags of green beans, ears of corn, turnips, tomatoes and heads of cabbage? This is only one of many unique experiences this pastor encountered during his 10 years of ministry as a circuit-riding preacher in the north woods of New England.

I just couldn't believe my eyes! They never told me anything about this in seminary. I couldn't get her under the water! Jill had wanted to be baptized by immersion, but there she was, one of the first people that I had led to the Lord in my new church, floating like a life raft in four and a half feet of water. If the wind had been blowing any harder, I would have had to pick her up on the other side of the lake.

Jill and her family had recently moved into town and

were in the process of joining one of our four yoked parish churches located near their home. It was a church that, by tradition, practiced infant baptism, but being transplanted Southern Baptists from Texas, this family requested that their daughter be baptized by immersion. Jill had recently made a profession of faith, asking Jesus into her heart as Lord and Saviour at one of our youth meetings, and as an ordained Baptist, I was more than happy to make the arrangements for this, my first baptism by immersion.

Considering this to be such a special occasion in their daughter's life, the family had chosen a special day for the baptism, Jill's parents' wedding anniversary. That was one of the key factors leading to the humor of the whole situation. Jill's parents had been married on the twenty-seventh of October and none of our four churches was equipped with a baptistry. That meant we would be going to the nearest lake, and in our neck of the woods the ponds may not be frozen over by the last week of October, but the trout know enough to go into hibernation for the winter. It wouldn't be necessary to cut a hole through the ice, but it wasn't going to be such a great day for a swim either.

I was surprised at the size of the crowd that had gathered along the shore on that particular October Sunday, but then I remembered that they had come to witness in their words, "The Dunking." Not only was this to be my first baptism by immersion, but it was to be their first as well. They had never witnessed such an event and we had three times as many people there for the baptism than had been in attendance in church earlier that morning.

But the size of the crowd didn't really bother me. After all, I was prepared. I had planned a simple but meaningful service. Not too formal for the occasion and setting, but still, it would be solemn and dignified. Jill and I stepped into the water and walked out from the shoreline until we were waist deep. I spoke of Jill's faith, her profession of love for Christ as her Saviour, and leaned her over backwards into the water, only to have her do a perfect imitation of a life raft drifting away in the breeze!

So much for the solemnity and dignity of the occasion. I put one hand on her head, one hand on her knees and pushed down as hard as I could. Hey, the next time you go to the beach, you try to hold an inflated life raft underwater and look dignified! *Slam dunk!*

Unknown to me, Jill had made some preparations for her own baptism that day. She may have been young and new to the area, but she was smart enough to figure out that the water in some of our local ponds often produced ice cubes by late October. Jill was determined not to get cold—or wet. She had wrapped a plastic trash bag around each leg and fastened them in place with rubber bands. She cut a hole in another bag and pulled it over her head, covering her body. She then completed the plastic ensemble with plastic bags securely fastened around each arm. When covered with her clothes and baptismal robe, she could not be recognized for what she was that day—a walking life raft, sincere in her faith, excited about her baptism, in love with the Lord and definitely unsinkable!

This was just one of a number of rather unique experiences that I was to encounter in 10 years of ministry as a northwoods circuit-riding preacher. I had been called right out of seminary at the age of 24 to pastor a unique combination of four churches representing three different denominations, the only Protestant churches ministering to four small towns nestled along a beautiful river valley in one of our New England states. It was this unique combination of diverse denominational affiliations and local church traditions that was often the source of a number of "firsts"—and I pray, "lasts"—in my ministry.

Consider, for instance, the first humorous incident in our ministry. My wife Karen reminds me however, that it wasn't quite as funny 13 years ago. In retrospect, who would have thought that a simple payday would result in so many tears?

After all, what could be so difficult about a simple payday? You don't have to be a seminary graduate to figure out what to do with a paycheck. You pick it up from your employer, endorse it on the back and take it to the bank. Easy enough, that is, if you get paid with money. But what if you get paid in veggies? How do you deposit a shopping bag full of fresh tomatoes in your bank account or turn a bag of freshly picked green beans into enough "green" to make a car payment?

That first payday was my initiation into the intricacies of our yoked parish and its 26 bank accounts. Each one of the four churches had its own church treasurer who paid the bills incurred by the local church and also sent money to the central parish treasurer who paid bills incurred by the parish as a whole. Simple enough, except that the bills were never split four ways. That would have been too easy.

If you're not confused yet, just wait a minute. I'm not done. Each church paid on a percentage basis, depending upon its percentage of total members in the parish, capital funds and property value. Our smallest church paid 13 percent, while the largest church paid 33 percent.

Confused now? It took me three years before I could figure out where I was supposed to be preaching on any given Sunday morning. And that first payday was even more confusing.

Prior to my arrival, the parish had been without a pastor for several months, meaning that none of the church treasurers had been sending money to the central parish treasurer. So when it came time to pay the preacher, not only was his cupboard bare, but the parish treasurer's was too. They had no money and I had no money, and we were both beginning to wonder what the pastor and his wife would be eating for the next two weeks.

That was when our resourceful parish treasurer came to the rescue. Perhaps she was inspired by the look of horror crossing my face as I contemplated two weeks of peanut butter-and-jelly sandwiches. She grabbed a handful of shopping bags, took me out to her garden and there it was. *Payday!* Enough green beans, ears of corn, turnips, tomatoes and cabbage to feed an army. All I had to do now was convince my wife that it was as good as cash.

I got about as far as the front door with that one. Karen took one look at the mixed bag of cabbage, brussels sprouts and beans, and as her eyes began to fill with tears I could barely hear her say, "What? No live chicken?"

It didn't take us long to discover that there were more than just a few things for which Karen and I had not been adequately prepared. Pickle-and-parsnip paydays proved to be difficult for Karen. Neither one of us had ever plucked a live chicken before, so we were lucky that a week of dinners from the garden was our only introduction to country living.

My introduction to the life and routine of a country pastor came a bit sooner. I didn't have to wait two weeks until my first payday to find out that being the pastor of the only Protestant churches serving four New England communities would carry a number of special responsibilities. I was introduced to the first of these within 48 hours of our arrival.

Karen and I completed the candidating procedure on Labor Day Sunday, as I preached to the combined congregations of the four parish churches and received a unanimous vote to become their pastor. That evening we stayed with Karen's parents. Then, because the parsonage had been rented out during the interim and the occupants had yet to begin looking for a new place to live, we moved on the following day, Labor Day, into the home of a parishioner and lived there for the next six weeks. We had not been in our temporary home for more than a few hours when I received a call from the local funeral director. He was calling to welcome me to the area with not one, but two funerals that week, one scheduled for the very next day and the other scheduled for Thursday.

I was a bit surprised because no one in the congregation had mentioned anything about the death of any of our church members, and it was at this point that I received my introduction to the routine and responsibilities of being the area's only Protestant preacher. The deceased were not members of my congregation, but they were not members of the local Roman Catholic church either, and that meant that I was expected to officiate at the services. I wasn't exactly sure what to say.

The problem was not whether I wanted to perform the services, but that I had never attended a funeral before in my life, much less performed one. I could parse verbs in Greek and Hebrew (though I barely remember the alphabets today), list the attributes of God, outline the Gospel of John from memory, lead a person to Christ and debate the intricacies of the faith. But bury the dead? Seminary had never prepared me for that, but prepared I had to be, for there were less than 24 hours to go before that first funeral service. I may not have learned about funerals in seminary, but I was determined that by the time I stepped behind the pulpit the following day, I would be ready.

It occurred to me that I had at least three things going in my favor: I could read, I had a friendly neighborhood funeral director at my disposal and I had a telephone. All three spelled out *help!* I turned to all three. The funeral director outlined a number of services that were commonly used by clergymen in that area of New England and I had the beginnings of my first funeral service.

I picked up the phone and called the pastor who had directed my final two years of supervised ministry while I was in seminary, and he added a number of pointers that gave me confidence that my first funeral would be one that the congregation would long remember. And then I read everything about funerals and funeral services that I could find—sample funeral sermons and book after book of pastoral funeral manuals with all of their helps and suggestions for conducting a funeral.

Tuesday came and this preacher was ready. I had the obituary to read, a number of appropriate Scripture readings, two or three meaningful poems and an outstanding message of comfort for the bereaved (all preachers think their messages are outstanding). I walked into the room, put my books down on the podium, prayed a silent prayer for strength and then looked out into the congregation only to discover that there *wasn't* a congregation. The room was empty except for me and the deceased!

It didn't take me long to discover why. I stepped into another room in the funeral home and cornered the funeral director only to learn that the reason there was no one present was because no one knew the deceased. Not a single person in that small town really knew the man. He had been a loner, living by himself in a rooming house for several months and had never made any friends. But that didn't matter according to the funeral director; the man was still dead and deserved a funeral.

I wasn't quite sure what to say. I had already heard the message I had prepared a half a dozen times the night before, and I was sure that the deceased really didn't care one way or the other. So I simply read a few passages of Scripture, offered a prayer and tucked the sermon away for Thursday. What a way to begin a ministry to those bowed down with grief. I had conducted my first funeral service and no one heard a word I had said. All I had was a captive audience. At least when I got home I would have no problem telling Karen who was there for the funeral and who wasn't. And who was to say that the service wasn't a success, after all? Not a single person complained!

About six weeks after my first funeral, Karen and I finally moved into our own home. The family that had been renting the parsonage had found a new place to live and now the parsonage was ours. Karen and I will always remember the day when we first moved into the home that we would later come to call "Overlook." Most of our friends thought that this nickname was a reference to the fact that our house was actually situated on the edge of a series of ledges and overlooked a beautiful river valley with a panoramic view of the mountains, but Karen and I knew better. We affectionately referred to the place as "Overlook" because we chose to overlook a few of it shortcomings.

Consider, for instance, the fact that someone had overlooked that a house needs doors, for, with the exception of the bathroom, there wasn't one in the whole house.

In the spring, we overlooked the running water in the cellar which usually forced us to overlook the lack of heat or hot water, because the furnace had disappeared in a seasonal flood. In the winter, we overlooked the need to look out the windows in the morning to see if it had snowed, because there would usually be a half-inch blanket of white on the kitchen floor. In cold weather the canned goods froze in the cabinets, my books froze to my study shelves, and there were occasions when Karen and I actually went outside to keep warm.

But it was our home and we loved it. We patched up the cracks in the floors that always told us if we had left a light on in the cellar, even from the bedroom on the second floor. We added insulation to the ceiling and walls and warmed up the rooms with carpeting and the fellowship of the wonderful friends who would become ours for a lifetime. One of the highlights that we would soon discover in that new home was the fellowship that we would have in the middle of the winter as we would gather for Bible study or for a visit around our new wood stove. It added warmth and beauty to our home, along with a lot of excitement to our lives.

After all this time, Karen and I will never forget the night that we had the first fire in our new wood stove—and in our living room and in our study and on the porch. The wood stove with beautiful white brickwork had been added to our home in order to keep the pastor and his wife warm on those cold fall and winter nights, and it was certainly responsible for heating things up in our lives. I built my first fire in the stove late one evening in October just before Karen and I went off to sleep. I knew that I would be up later on that evening for Karen was eight months pregnant with our first child and had a built-in alarm clock of her own. I would take that opportunity to check the stove.

Sure enough, her alarm went off at two in the morning and as she went down to visit the bathroom, I went to visit my stove. I worked over the coals and added a fresh supply of wood, all without ever opening my eyes. I had to have them shut because, if they had been open, I would have noticed a few things out of the ordinary, like the fact that the wallpaper above the stove had been burned to a crisp and there was smoke pouring through the wall in my study. At least Karen was a bit more alert and she sounded the alarm. The house was on fire!

Most people would have called the fire department, but we argued. Even with all that smoke I wasn't convinced that the house was really on fire. And when she did convince me, we discovered that we had no idea who to call. I didn't know the number of the fire department; I didn't know the number of the police department. But I did know the number of the Forest Fire Warden who just happened to be a deacon in the church. I really lucked out for his wife was the one who was supposed to call all the members of the volunteer fire department.

He arrived only to be greeted with an earful of questions: How long would it take for the fire trucks to get there? Should we start dragging furniture out of the house? Would it be a good idea for me to take the six boxes of shotgun shells and two pounds of black powder out of the cabinet mounted on the wall that was now on fire (city slickers sometimes ask silly questions).

He took one look at the smoke and flames, hollered, "Get me some water" and began attacking the wall paneling with a crowbar. Karen and I both arrived back at the study three minutes later. I had hitched a hose to the kitchen faucet and was trailing water through the kitchen, dining room and hallway. Karen arrived with a glass of cold water from the bathroom. She thought the man was thirsty. Would you believe the fire warden expelled both of us from the scene?

Yes, the volunteer fire department did arrive in record time, in less than 10 minutes at two in the morning. The house was saved and we all ended up with a good laugh as it didn't take long for the story about the glass of water to make its rounds. Later on that evening, we met for a regularly scheduled church business meeting and listened to the church clerk as she read from the minutes of the last meeting, "It was voted to install a wood stove in the parsonage in order to keep the pastor and his wife warm." The first fire went into the church records as one that we would all remember for a long time.

Not only was that first parsonage home to Karen and our growing family, it was also the center of a growing ministry to our four churches and to our community. None of our churches was heated during the week, nor did any of them have a telephone or space for an office or study. Our home was centrally located within the parish and heated to some degree in the winter, making it the logical site for many a church meeting.

Deacons met in our living room, and regularly scheduled Bible studies took place around our wood stove, now repaired and safely functioning as long as the wind didn't blow. Informal gatherings took place around the coffeepot, and the valley's only piano recitals took place around our piano. Our spare bedroom housed a multitude of individuals ranging from guest speakers to stranded hikers passing through the area in the spring and summer. The study was just the right size for youth meetings, and our kitchen was transformed into the kindergarten Sunday School classroom on Sunday mornings. The living room was the message center for the church and our phone, the church phone.

All of this meant that Karen was required to wear a number of hats. Not only was she busy raising two children with an often absent husband, but she also cleared the breakfast dishes in record time for Sunday School, answered the phone and took messages for those trying to track down the circuit-riding preacher—I did a lot of riding, 33,000 miles the first year—and often did a better job at giving out advice than the preacher. But most important of all, Karen developed a superb sense of timing when it came to disappearing while I held counseling sessions. She had little choice since my office was without a door. She knew exactly when to leave for a last-minute trip to the grocery store, arriving back home just as my visitor would be going out the door.

Our home was, in fact, the location of my very first session of premarital counseling. After all that time and money spent on pastoral counseling classes in seminary, I would finally have the opportunity to do something in ministry for which I had been trained. I think I was more excited about the pending marriage than the bride and groom! I spent the whole week before the scheduled session going over my notes from class and reviewing every Norman Wright book on marriage counseling that I owned. In no time at all I had five counseling sessions outlined and ready to go. I had finally solved the greatest debate I could remember having in seminary: How many premarital counseling sessions should a pastor have, four or six?

I was ready to tie a knot that would never come undone. I was ready to offer the solution to all of the problems that a married couple could face in the next 10 years. If they were unsaved, I'd get 'em saved. If they had a rocky foundation, I'd make it solid.

Their car turned into the driveway just as Karen pulled out for a quick trip to the grocery store—another gallon of milk whether we needed it or not. I just had to do something about getting a door on that study before we went broke. The couple walked into the living room as we introduced ourselves and by the time we had settled into the study, I was rarin' to go.

Ann was a local girl in her 20s living just a few miles from our home with a good job in a nearby college town. Her fiancé, Richard was about 10 years older, an impressive-looking man dressed that evening in a pinstriped business suit that made me a bit curious about his line of work as we didn't see too many business suits out our way. I'm almost sorry today that I even asked. His answer sort of took the wind out of my sails and crushed my dreams as an up-and-coming, hot-shot counselor. He was a professor at the local state university with a Ph.D. in Psychology and taught—you guessed it, folks— *Counseling.*

So much for my outline; so much for my five sessions. It wasn't that I felt intimidated or anything like that, but I vaguely remember muttering something like, "Gee, that sounds interesting. What kind of wedding service did you have in mind?" as I slipped 12 pages of notes and two counseling books into the trash can beneath my desk. I was eager and rarin' to do some counseling, but not that eager. Maybe another opportunity would come for me to put those things I had learned in seminary into action.

It wasn't long in coming either. Our home was the location of my first counseling session—some counseling session! And our neighborhood was to be the location of my first fight. No, I don't mean a theological debate, an apologetic kind of fight, I mean a real knockdown, throw-a-left-hook, kind of fight. I didn't go looking for it, but it sort of found me as I exercised my circuit-riding duties.

I had just arrived home late one Friday afternoon following not one, but two wedding rehearsals. Saturday would be a busy day with a small wedding in the morning and, later that afternoon, for a young lady who had gone through our youth fellowship and was a recent college graduate, one of the largest weddings I had ever performed. I had no sooner stepped out of the car when I became aware of a number of things at the same time. Karen was waiting for me on the front step with a look of concern on her face while, at the same time, my ears picked up the sound of a loud argument coming from up the road. Karen informed me that this couple, new to our area, had been arguing on their front porch for nearly an hour, and from the sounds of it we knew it must be serious. Actually it sounded more than serious, for someone was in real trouble. Not only did we hear screaming, but we could hear the sounds of someone being beaten. Karen ran inside to call the police while I ran up the road to see if I could help.

I arrived on the spot to find a young lady on the ground being beaten and kicked by a young man who appeared to be a bit strung out. I had no problem getting him to leave her alone because he had found another target on which to vent his anger: me. Not only was I interfering in a family matter (he was in the process of "disciplining" his wife, which he said, was no business of mine), but also I was trespassing on his property. I had about four and a half seconds to leave or trade places with his wife.

Now there's an occasion that they never prepare you for in seminary. Boxing 101, anyone? That's exactly what I needed, because I wasn't about to leave until the police arrived. I stood my ground (it was really his ground and I was trespassing) as he grabbed me by the front of my shirt and pulled back his fist. The only thing I could think of was my two weddings the next day. "Lord," I prayed, "don't let him break anything I need for tomorrow!"

And the Lord must have heard or else this guy was a lot better at beating his wife than he was at beating me. He swung and I ducked. I lost the buttons off the front of my shirt and about four ounces of skin off my chest as his knuckles relieved me of about two layers of flesh and left me with a scar that I still bear today. And all of this just as the police cruiser pulled into his driveway. I left the scene as the police took the man into custody (his wife later declined to press charges), and I went home thankful that I had all of my speaking parts in place and functioning for the following day's nuptials.

Later that evening I sat in the darkness of the living room sorting out the events of the day. All I could think of was a life verse that I had chosen for the ministry. With the apostle Paul I had been committed to saying, "I have become all things to all men so that by all possible means I might save some" (I Cor. 9:22). But Lord, I didn't know that this "all things" business included becoming a punched-out preacher!

At least Karen and I now had an open door for witnessing to our new neighbor, but what a way to break the ice. We spent hours in ministry to that young mother and her children. Her husband soon left her and years later was killed in a tragic set of circumstances which came about as a result of his temper. But even today, years after the incident, that young lady and her children live "just up the road" from our first home, the heart of so much of our ministry to a people that we grew to love and cherish.

Not only was our first home the site of much excitement in our lives as I carried on a ministry from my office, kitchen table and front porch, but it was also the site of much excitement even when I was away. My first evening away from home and my family stands out clearly in my mind, even today, because that was the night that George came calling, gun and all.

I had met George several months earlier on a Sunday morning. He was a quiet, well-dressed man in his 50s who came as a visitor to one of our worship services. I made it a point to speak with him following the service and learned that George was new to our area and looking for a place to live. He was presently staying at one of our local motels, so I made an appointment to join him for breakfast the next morning in hopes that I might be an encouragement to him as he looked for a more permanent home and job.

I soon learned that George had a few problems: the next day he called me 17 times between breakfast and lunch! He was calm one minute and almost violent the next. He talked about his experiences in the Korean war, his love for music, his desire to cut all bonds with his family. He would talk for hours on the subject of German chocolate cake. He caused considerable trouble at local restaurants, chased people out of stores and each time he got into any kind of trouble, he called me. Karen got to the point where she wouldn't even go near the phone. But it kept on ringing.

His last call came at midnight. He was stranded 30 miles away in a fairly large town. Anything in our neck of the woods with a population over 2,000 was known as

"The Big City." He had been drinking and was afraid that he might end up in jail. He had no money and no way to get back to his motel room. Would it be possible for me to come and pick him up? It was either that or listen to the phone ring all night long!

Karen made some remark about which one of us was the craziest and insisted that if I went, at least I could take someone with me. It would be the perfect opportunity to let one of our deacons in on life in the ministry. I picked up the phone and called Gary, the chairman of our diaconate, who agreed to make the trip with me. It was a night that he would never forget! George sat in the back seat all the way home and was just short of violent. Gary had brought along a bag of chips to munch on the trip and kept stuffing them into George's mouth. At least he was polite enough not to rant and rave with his mouth full.

An hour later we finally dropped George off at his motel room where he was met by the police. Early the next morning he was given a one-way bus ticket back to his hometown, but that was not the last we were to see of George. We were not to forget him nor was he to forget, of all people, me.

Shortly after George arrived in his hometown, he was arrested for causing a disturbance and was placed in a local hospital for observation. At least with George under that kind of care, I could get back to my ministry and some of the other plans that I had made, such as the all-night youth rally and bowling party that our church group would be attending 50 miles away—the closest bowling alley we could find.

I was just about to walk out the front door for my first night away from home and my family when the phone rang. It was the chief of police; George had escaped from the institution. They knew that he had a gun, and guess who they thought he was coming to visit!

I wasn't sure what to do. I was afraid to leave my family, and at the same time I was in charge of a program for over a hundred young people that night. The chief of police knew of my dilemma and came to the rescue in the form of a police cruiser, complete with flashing lights, parked in my driveway from six P.M. until I arrived home the next morning.

We never saw George again, at least alive. Several months later I received another call from the police. A body had been discovered in the woods by a group of local hunters. The man had hanged himself and the police thought that it might be George. Could I come by and help with the identification? I recognized his backpack, his pocket New Testament, a small vial of holy water that he always carried and his favorite bean pot. It was George. A lonely man had come to an even more lonely end. The only person that he ever harmed was himself.

Karen and I had been involved in a ministry to the four churches of our parish for about eight years when they decided to merge into one and build a centrally-located church building within walking distance from our home. The merger of those four churches and the construction of the new building was a first in itself for me and, I pray, Dear Lord, the last. The planning, merging and construction was filled with incidents that we would never forget. Of all the incidents involved in the building of the new church, including the raising of the finances and the dedication and worship in the new sanctuary, our first baptismal service in a brand-new baptistry stands out in my mind.

Now, you may be under the impression that I was jinxed when it came to baptisms, but that's not true. Ever since that first baptism by immersion with Jill, I had been baptizing new believers with regularity in anything that held water. In warm weather we held baptismal services in the local lakes and ponds and, on several occasions, in the river. During the winter we baptized our new believers in an indoor swimming pool at a local resort hotel. We struggled with the question as to whether or not chlorinated water was holy, but figured that it was better than chopping holes in the ice in the middle of February. With the exception of that first baptism and the one lady that I almost lost in the current when we were baptizing in the river, the rest went smoothly.

But now, my troubles were over. Our new church was equipped with a brand-new, handy-dandy, fiberglass, aqua-blue baptistry, complete with an electric water circulator and heating unit! Now that was real class. I couldn't wait to try it out.

We had been in the new building for only a few weeks when that opportunity finally came. A number of new believers requested baptism by immersion, and we planned the service for the next Sunday evening. A little anxious, I came into the church early on Friday morning, filled the tank and turned on the circulator and water heater only to find out that absolutely nothing worked. The heater ran for about two seconds and turned off. I was ready to cry; my new toy was broken.

I called an emergency meeting of a number of men for later that evening in my new church office—complete with door and telephone. We pulled out the blueprints for the baptistry and heating unit, grabbed a box of tools and went to work. Between the six of us we discovered the problem, none of the wires to the heating unit sensor had been connected. By the time we finished that night, the wires were in place and the water was flowing smoothly through the circulator. By Sunday, the water would be just right.

Only I was wrong about that one. We may have gotten the wires in place, but they were not in the right place. The circulator ran smoothly and the water heated and heated and heated. It heated all through Friday evening, all day on Saturday and all through that night. By the time I walked into the church on Sunday morning I was greeted by a steam bath and a bubbling baptistry. The heater was connected, but not in a way that it could shut off. The water was hot enough to boil lobsters.

By the time we were ready for the service on Sunday evening, the water had cooled down to about 90 degrees. The second I stepped into the baptistry dressed in my rubber waders, I realized that the temperature was to be the least of my problems. We had boiled away about a foot of water, so it was now a bit shallow, but it also appeared that I had forgotten about something else: the grease and oil that we were supposed to rinse out of the circulator and heating unit. To say that the bottom of the tank was slick would be putting it mildly. I was going to have to dig in all 10 toes just to keep from going under myself. And you should have seen the oil floating on the top of the water. Scum city! Not only were these folks going to be baptized that night, they were going to be anointed as well!

The service began at seven and seemed to be going smoothly, until I came to Jean. She was tall and the water was shallow and I had an idea that she might be trouble, but when she came up out of the water, I just couldn't believe that I had dunked her and left so much dry. Just as I leaned her back into the water, she tucked in her chin and everything went under except from her eyebrows on up. I missed the whole top of her head! But I was determined;

this was my first baptism in the new baptistry and I was going to do it right. So before Jean could get away, I baptized her again, right down to the bottom of the tank.

Later on that week as I filled out the baptismal certificates, I made out two for Jean. One was completely filled out, but I left the top half of the second one blank.

One year after the dedication of that new church building, Karen and I accepted a call to a church in a different part of New England. It was difficult to make the decision to leave our first church with so many memories and friends, but we felt that our ministry there was complete and that God was directing us to a new field. As I reflect upon that experience of 10 years of ministry, I believe that God used it as an opportunity to teach me just how much I needed to depend upon Him and the resources with which He had surrounded me.

I learned the importance of working hand in hand with a fine congregation who were actually partners in ministry, having been gifted by God and equipped by their shepherd to do works of service. Our state-wide fellowship of pastors was another source of strength to my personal life, as we met on a regular basis for fellowship and to share what we had been learning in ministry. I also began to realize that in spite of what I may have said from time to time, seminary did prepare me for ministry. My years of training had taught me to think on my feet and to use my mind in creative ways.

But most of all, my experience in my first church taught me just how much I needed to depend on the Holy Spirit of God as my guide and source of strength and knowledge. As long as I depended upon myself, my attempts to minister to others would remain a struggle and would often end in failure. When I relied upon God and His

Son for my source of wisdom, He would lead me to make those right decisions that would allow me to effectively minister for Him.

I had been in my new church for only a few weeks when I was faced with a decision that called for much prayer and guidance from the Spirit. I received a telephone call to go back to my first church to minister to a special need. It was a difficult decision, because it involved someone who was so special to me. That young lady, Jill, who had provided so much excitement and delight at my first baptism, had been found murdered. Would I consider coming back to perform the funeral service?

It was a decision with which I wrestled, for I had promised myself and the interim pastor that I would not go back for any reason. I did not want to set a precedent which might take away from the effectiveness of the ministry of any pastor who was to follow me in that north-country ministry. My heart cried out to go back, to comfort those whom I cared for and loved, but my spirit said no. I would not go back as a pastor, to conduct a funeral service. But several weeks later, I allowed myself to go back to visit the family as I wanted to and needed to—as their friend.

How Do *You* Identify?

Have you ever heard the words, "Be Prepared"? Not in reference to the Boy Scout Motto, but an exhortation given by the apostle Paul to his brother in the faith, Timothy. "Preach the Word; be prepared in season and out of season; correct, rebuke and encourage—with great patience and careful instruction" (2 Tim. 4:2).

Be prepared in season and out of season. Does that

mean that in order for someone to be truly effective in ministry he must ski with the deacons in the winter, fish with visitors in the spring, play golf with members of the church board in the summer and hunt with prospective new members in the fall? Is it God's plan for effective ministry to be patterned after the American sportsman? Although Paul may have wholeheartedly approved of such an approach to ministry, he had something else in mind when he wrote his letter to Timothy.

"Be prepared" because the world around you is just full of surprises and opportunities for any believer to bear witness through personal ministry. And no seminary education will ever prepare you for what life will eventually present in terms of crisis and challenge. It is in this light that pastors and parishioners are on equal ground. Both are often just as effective (or ineffective) in specific situations because neither have been "professionally prepared." Yet, each one of us can "Be Prepared."

The first step in our effort to "Be Prepared" comes as we acknowledge complete dependence upon the Holy Spirit in all our efforts to serve God. In order to do this, both pastor and lay person must be willing to walk closely with the Lord. Very often, those hard to handle situations seem to arise in those times when Bible study and prayer time have been squeezed out of a busy schedule. It could really be that these situations are not all that difficult to handle, but that we are out of touch enough with the Lord that we can't quite hear His voice giving direction when most needed.

Second, each member of the body needs to depend upon the gifts and talents of other members of the Body. That in itself is one of the most unique characteristics of the Body, human or spiritual. Paul reminds us that, "The body is a unit, though it is made up of many parts; and though all its parts are many, they form one body" (1 Cor. 12:12). Each of those parts have different functions, but each is needed by the other so that the Body might work together as a whole.

God has surrounded us with a storehouse of talent. Take time to look and you may find someone right next to you on Sunday morning who has gone through a similar problem as the one you may be presently experiencing. And yet, for many, the tendency is to take the "Lone Ranger" approach. We have been called into a leadership role or have been asked by a friend to solve a problem, a family member has come to us with a need, and somehow we find ourselves stuck. We need to turn to other brethren to ask for help. Members of the Body had better begin to realize that we need each other, for the sake of the Body and for the sake of God's kingdom.

Finally, never be surprised! You may be caught by surprise, but be assured God can use any event, any situation and set of circumstances, painful or painfully amusing, to bring honor and glory to Himself. What a privilege it is for each one of us to be used by God in the wonderful work of His Church and His Kingdom.

6

God's Power in My Weakness

He was a pastor; he was a husband; he was a father. And, he was an alcoholic. Certainly not the standard combination we expect to find in the pastorate. But here is a man who had, because of his drinking problem, become bankrupt physically, spiritually and mentally. How could something like this happen to a pastor? When did it all begin? And what would become of this minister of God's Word?

Alcoholism. What does that word conjure up in your mind? A skid-row bum, smelly, dirty, unshaven, filthy clothes, sunken eyes and all the other things you associate with depraved fallen humanity? You wouldn't say a seminary graduate ministering to a local church is a likely candidate to be classified as an alcoholic, would you?

I'll call myself Walter—Walter the alcoholic. But wait, there's more to a description of me than that—I'm also minister of a small church in Somewhere, U.S.A. That could be in your town. I'm for real; the only thing unreal about me is my name.

I'll never forget what, I hope, was my last drunken spree. It was May 14, 1983. I had spent a typical Saturday morning putting the finishing touches on my sermon. The next day I was preaching on addictions. Can you imagine an alcoholic minister of the gospel having the nerve to preach on that subject? I still find it hard to believe.

As usual, Saturday afternoon was spent drinking whiskey with beer chasers while I mowed the lawn and weeded the garden. That evening I went to the First and Last Chance Saloon for a couple of beers before retiring for the evening. It was my first, and hopefully last, time in that particular establishment. It was a dull, unfriendly place so I didn't stay long. As I look back on it, I think I may have been the one who was dull and unfriendly.

The next morning came and I was *moachus* as usual. You won't find *moachus* in the dictionary, but just about every alcoholic knows the word. It is the state of being nearly senseless—in a fog. I also had feelings of dread and remorse, but they disappeared after a quick breakfast and the 40-mile ride to my country church.

People filled the sanctuary with happy expectancy and cheerful chatter. I preached a strong sermon on addictions, admonishing the congregation to defile not the body, which is the "temple of the Holy Spirit" (1 Cor. 6:19, *NASB*).

Following the service, I sauntered into Fellowship Hall, tinkled a bell for silence and said grace. As I poured myself a cup of coffee, a young man watched me closely and exclaimed, "Your hand is shaking!"

"What?" I replied, startled.

"Your hand is shaking," he repeated.

I'd heard him the first time but was trying to think of a response. "I have hypoglycemia," I stammered. "It's a low-blood-sugar condition and one of the symptoms is shaking."

He just looked at me and walked away. I haven't seen him in church since.

That confrontation was like a trapdoor opening under my feet. I was falling through, collapsing within myself like the walls of Jericho. I had told a half-truth; I do have a mild case of hypoglycemia. But I don't think that young man was convinced. The important thing is that *I* was not convinced. At that moment the truth struck me that I was an alcoholic. My sermon was applicable to me more than anyone else in the congregation. "Physician, heal thyself" (Luke 4:23, *KJV*)!

For about a month I went without alcohol but had no serenity. I was edgy, irritable and argumentative. At one point my wife Peg and I were arguing while I was doing the dishes. To dramatize my point, I threw a handful of silverware on the floor. When I did that, however, a bread knife stuck into Peg's foot, and I had to rush her to the hospital. I could see the headlines: "Baptist Minister Stabs Wife in Foot."

Peg received three stitches and there were no headlines. Nevertheless, I feared hurting her again, so I went to the ocean for a couple of days to think. When I returned, Peg handed me the book, *Under the Influence*. It discussed, among other things, the relationship of hypoglycemia to alcoholism, and repeatedly urged alcoholics to get involved in Alcoholics Anonymous (AA). I finished the book and joined the AA group in my town all in the same evening.

At the meeting, I admitted that I am an alcoholic. Several men gave me their phone numbers in case I felt the urge to drink or just needed to talk. One went over the schedule of meetings with me, indicating which would be best to attend. I've been active in that group ever since and feel very much at home there. By the grace of God I have not had a drink or a substitute in over two years.

I don't know if I ever was just a social drinker. My experience was that I usually got drunk, sometimes sick and passed out. Occasionally, I had blackouts. I can't remember leaving the scene of one party, although I do recollect being carried into my apartment.

A lot of energy has been invested in reconstructing my life, as well as seeking to understand my periodic fits of bizarre behavior. Much assistance in this endeavor has come through Alcoholics Anonymous, as well as participation in an Adult Children of Alcoholics workshop.

How do I know I am an alcoholic? Looking back over the past 10 years, I recall many attempts to control my drinking without success. For a few weeks I actually limited my drinking to only one day a week, my racquetball day. After sweating off two to three pounds in a couple of hours, nothing tasted better than cool pitchers of beer, one after the other.

Although I was controlling my drinking to one day a week, I was still drinking to an excess when I did drink. Also, I could never tell Peg when I would be home for supper. It varied from 6:00 P.M. to 11:00 P.M., usually depending on how good the beer was tasting. Sometimes I wouldn't get home until the next morning.

Before long, I decided that I needed more than one day a week of exercise, so I began playing racquetball Mondays and Wednesdays. Now I was drinking two days a week. Soon I added Fridays to my sport-drinking routine, after which I realized that I was only kidding myself, so I resumed my daily drinking pattern.

During another period, I had progressed from drinking beer to drinking whiskey—scotch and bourbon—in measured amounts. I would make a mark on the label of the fifths with the intention of drinking only to the designated point for a day's libation. When I reached the mark, I usually wanted more, so I would defiantly make another mark to drink down to. After all, who made the mark to begin with? Who is the one in control anyway? Not I, that's for sure!

Nevertheless, with typical denial, I insisted I was not an alcoholic—we are just about the last ones to know. For one thing, I did not wear a long dirty trench coat and sleep in alleyways. I did not miss work due to alcoholism. In fact, during my last year of drinking, when I still combined teaching with ministry, I was cited by my school superintendent for perfect attendance. Evaluation by my superiors was always good-to-excellent, and I served effectively as coordinator and English department head for a period of seven years.

Another thing I never did was drink before noon, because I knew only alcoholics drank in the mornings. I never had auto mishaps and never went to jail or the hospital as a result of my drinking.

Often were the times I could drink all night and show little effects, while others passed out or became ill. I prided myself on my tolerance, but now I know that my body had merely accommodated itself to the foreign poison of alcohol. In total reality, I was sicker than the ones who passed out!

When I drank I thought I was charming, witty and good company. If I was, that all ran out when I became spiritually, mentally and physically bankrupt. Only *I* thought I was witty. At a party, one teacher turned to her husband and said, "Isn't he funny?"

His reply was "I feel sorry for him."

One reason I remember those words was that they coincided with my own feelings about myself. I had thought I was charming, but now I remember women refusing to dance with me or reluctantly doing so— probably afraid I might say or write something funny or humiliating about them if they refused. I wasn't very good company either!

What's a good minister like me doing being an alcoholic? A minister needs to set a good moral example and we all know that alcoholism results in excessive drinking which is sin, not to mention other moral ramifications of the unruly life of an alcoholic.

First, I need to say that alcoholism is defined by the American Medical Association as a disease, although the Church usually focuses on the moral and social dimensions. In other words, I have a disease called alcoholism, which has resulted in spiritual, physical and cerebral impairment.

Physically, I ended up shaking a lot and using two hands to unlock my car door. My mild hypoglycemia, which seems to act up under stress, was also a related symptom. Now that I am no longer drinking and have modified my life-style, I can eat practically anything without the shakes, blurred vision or narcolepsy (attacks of deep sleep). In fact, the physical damages of alcohol are the quickest to mend. A few years ago, I was refused insurance because of high blood pressure. Now it registers around 120 over 80.

The effect of alcohol on the brain is another matter, however. It is generally believed that it takes two to five years of abstinence for the alcoholic to recover anything like clear thinking. After two years, I can already notice the difference. Before, my mental distress came in the form of anxiety attacks.

One day while reading to my eighth grade English class, I suddenly felt dizzy and faint. I could no longer read, so I appointed a student to continue while I retreated in fear and panic to the teachers' room. Alone, I puzzled over my plight for about five minutes and returned to the class feeling shaky, but able to carry on.

For seven years, similar attacks would strike on a daily basis. They would be triggered by circumstances, such as walking down a long crowded corridor, speaking to a class or group, reading a long paragraph aloud, being with authoritative people or serious people, ad infinitum.

I saw doctors, psychiatrists, psychologists and social workers. No one could find anything wrong with me. When asked if I drank, I would say, "Yes, moderately."

I read self-help books, including *The Male Mid-Life Crisis: Fresh Starts After 40, Passages, Self-Realization and Self-Defeat, Be the Person You Were Meant to Be, Pulling Your Own Strings, Sugar Blues* and many others.

The anxieties continued as long as I drank and even into my months of sobriety. This experience provides an important lesson: one's problems don't end the moment one gives up drinking. A lot has been set in motion by years of drinking that haunts us in our sobriety.

Drinking also hurt me spiritually. I tailor-made my religious thinking to accommodate my life-style of daily drinking. For instance, I changed affiliation to a denomination where drinking was more acceptable. We often had wine and cheese after choir rehearsal at the new church. I drank too much, but so did others, so I didn't feel so different.

In my preaching, I often proclaimed that the Bible does not condemn moderate drinking. I still believe that, but what I was doing was wrong. I was using the Bible as a rationale for a life-style that had actually gone out of control.

I became very ecumenical and learned to appreciate the perspectives of other faiths. I think this in itself is commendable, but my motivation was the self-centered desire to run away from a personal God, as Adam had done after disobeying God (see Gen. 3). I began to think and speak about God in nebulous, impersonal terms, such as ground of all being, ultimate concern, unmoved mover, nirvana and others. I had lost contact with my personal God who has revealed Himself as Father, Son and Holy Spirit.

So alcohol had led to my becoming bankrupt physically, spiritually and mentally. It is truly a threefold disease.

But, how did this illness start? I am responsible for my own alcoholism and can't blame my parents, but they are a part of my story. I believe I had the "ism" long before I took the alcohol. In other words, I had the personality and character of an alcoholic long before I took my first drink.

Alcoholism is a family disease. It affects every member adversely, bringing personality and character damage to all. Educational family alcoholism workshops emphasize that children and grandchildren are hurt by the presence of even one alcoholic in the family.

My first years were spent in a family like TV's Ozzie

and Harriet Nelson's or the families on *My Three Sons* and *Leave It to Beaver.* We were a model American family. Dad worked as a foreman for H.P. Hood and put his week's pay on the kitchen table every Thursday afternoon. Envelopes were then stuffed with the proper amounts for rent, insurance, groceries and other expenses. Mom would walk all over town to pay respective creditors.

We were always on time for supper, at 5:30 P.M., and we ate as a family. The meal would always include meat, vegetable, potatoes and dessert. For awhile we even had our own garden and chickens.

When I began school I was also sent to Sunday School at First Baptist Church. It was our baby-sitter who saw to it that we got there. I liked the teachers and the Bible stories they told. When I was 12 I gave my life to Jesus and was baptized. The New Testament I received from the church had Romans 8:28 on the inside front cover: "And we know that all things work together for good to them that love God, to them who are the called according to his purpose" (*KJV*). That became my life verse, and I have seldom doubted its truth in spite of the direction my life has taken.

On Sunday afternoons my brother Bud and I would go to the movies. When we came home the whole family would lie on the big bed listening to "Nick Carter, Master Detective," "Edgar Bergen and Charlie McCarthy" and a number of other favorite radio programs. We ate homemade fudge and popcorn, and felt warm and secure.

Unfortunately, the good times did not roll on. Toward the end of World War II with its blackouts and rationing, we moved closer to where Dad worked, from the country to the city.

It seemed that Dad and Mom were out every night.

We certainly went through a lot of baby-sitters. Later I discovered that my parents were spending a lot of time at a drinking establishment in Salem, Massachusetts called The Silver Slipper. Dad would sleep in the afternoon and be out late at night with Mom. Mealtimes became punctuated with frightening arguments, and Dad would throw his plate on the floor if he did not like the food. Things around our house became a little like "All in the Family"!

The situation began to worsen. Toward the end, Bud and I would often be interrupted out of a sound sleep at two or three in the morning by bitter arguments. Mom would call us into the kitchen to be witnesses in case Dad tried to hurt her. One night, Dad was bleeding from his nose and forehead after Mom apparently had hit him with a heavy glass candlestick. He needed three stitches in his nose. Things were now like "Hill Street Blues" around the house.

My grades in school went from *A*'s to *C*'s. I daydreamed often, shoplifted with the neighborhood kids and beat up on my brother. If a friend stayed overnight at my house, we would simply tip my brother out of his bed and let him continue his sleep on the floor. I didn't care much about myself or other people. I already had the "ism" of alcoholism before I ever touched a drop.

I went to three different schools during seventh grade. That was the year my father and mother were divorced. I came home from my last day in the sixth grade to find my clothes and many of our household goods packed on a pickup truck. My mother informed us that we were leaving my father, so I took seat cushions from the living room furniture, put them in the bathtub and filled the tub with water. I'm still not sure why I did that.

My brother and I went to Maine to live with Mom and

a skinny man we had never seen before. He put sugar on my potatoes once when I was teasing my brother, so I didn't like him very much. I liked him even less when I discovered him making love to Mother and found filthy poems that he had written about her. That summer was one drinking party after another in a crowded house full of lewd, noisy men. One night I broke the screen near my bed and went to sleep in the woods.

That September, during supper, the outside door was kicked in and there stood Dad and a sheriff, with guns pointed at us. We went back to Salem to live with Dad who had gotten legal custody. I resented my mother for not making any attempt to keep us or for not showing much remorse about our having to leave.

I became a depressed, quiet teenager. During school lunch, I would stay in and just stare out the window. I liked working at setting up pins in a bowling alley, however, and I liked the youth group in our church. I liked driving too. Dad taught me how when I was 13, so I could become his taxi service to bars and women. By the time I was 16, I didn't want to live.

One night I chose to walk home from BYF, our youth group, rather than accept a ride. I wanted to be alone to talk with God. I had walked about half the 10 miles home when I looked up at the stars and addressed my Maker. I told Him I was tired of my life, and I wanted Him to take it. I was so sincere in this prayer, I fully expected to have a fatal heart attack or have lightning out of a cloudless sky strike me.

What happened was something I never expected: A flood of joy and peace filled me from head to toe. I wanted to knock on the doors of strangers and tell them God loved them. I believed at that moment God called me to become a minister of the gospel. Just then a carload of fellow BYF'ers came along and took me the rest of the way home. I enthusiastically told them what had happened to me on that back road. How did they know I was taking that road home? I didn't think to ask them.

When I told my father I was going to be a minister, he said he would vomit in his pew if he ever heard me. I guess he didn't think I was a good enough person to be a minister. But that did not discourage me. I was too full of enthusiasm at this new direction in my life.

I initiated table grace at our supper meals, but got a little static from Dad. Once he interrupted me to say, "Don't thank God. Thank me. I'm the one who earned the money." I still didn't have a good relationship with Dad.

I sent tracts to my mother and she was offended. My brother, I think, was simply confused about what was going on with me. I felt as if I no longer had a family in the biological sense, but I was keenly aware that I was a part of the family of God.

I enrolled at a Christian college, on probation, since I had not taken college preparatory courses in high school. Leaving home at 17, I worked my way through, starting college in 1955 and graduating in 1963 with a B.Ed. During those eight years, my father died of alcoholism, I flunked out of my first college, got married and fathered four of our five boys, attended two other colleges and began drinking. I decided I wanted to drink more than I wanted to be a minister.

In the summer of 1963, following the advice of drinking companions, I began seeing a psychologist. After several sessions, he challenged me to follow through on my call to be a minister and attend seminary, which I did, receiving my degree in three years, without touching a drop of alcohol. I was a teaching assistant in the Old and New Testament departments and master of ceremonies at our graduation banquet, a truly successful period in my life.

Decision time had arrived. Should I go to Harvard for more graduate work or become pastor of a local church? I took the church, resolving to return to theological study later. In 1966, a small association of churches ordained me, and I rushed down to my post a month before they thought they were ready for me. In a year and a half, I resumed drinking, alienating several church people who would not do what I told them to do, and I ran off to the west coast with a young lady who was the BYF president.

Now why would a well-educated family man throw away his career and family to go to California with a 17-year-old? The cunning, baffling disease called alcoholism.

We returned from California so I could be near my children. I took a position as a public school teacher. By this time I was a daily drinker, mainly beer. I loved parties, drinking after bowling, tennis and racquetball, and I loved having 25 to 80 people at a time partying at my house. I thought I was living. After five years of this, my sweetheart walked out on me and gave me my second divorce. There was no feeling of remorse, only relief that I could drink as I wished with no one to nag me.

Drinking enabled me to escape feeling. It covered over pain, fear, loneliness, inferiority, anxiety, rejection, insecurity and a host of other feelings. In time I became so numb that the only feelings I was able to experience were depression and excitement. I needed to do outrageous things to prove to myself that I was still alive.

One night a drinking companion and I staged a mock argument as we closed up a drinking establishment. We argued on the way out and he shot me with a blank pistol. I fell behind a parked car which had begun to back up. I got out of the way just in time.

On another occasion, a fellow department head and I decided to disrobe in front of our principal and mixed company, and go out to play streaker tennis. The court was locked up, so at midnight the phantom streakers played tennis in the street. The next day, one of my students told me he had seen me play streaker tennis. He was proud of me, he said. I guess we were not the only sick ones!

I haven't had a drink now for just over two years, but I can look back and see what I lost due to alcohol. I lost two wives, five children, two houses full of furniture, one automobile, untold thousands of dollars, two professions and a department-head position, innumerable friends and acquaintances. I lost my mental, physical and spiritual health and well-being. I lost years of potential growth and character development, and I missed seeing my children grow up.

Before I end my story, I want to share what I've gained through sobriety with the help of Alcoholics Anonymous and God. With Christ in my life, as I work my AA program, I don't have to drink again. The AA program works for me because its principles—those of the 1833 Oxford Movement in England—can produce a spiritual awakening within one. And such an awakening has been my experience.

An alcoholic must, first of all, admit he is powerless over alcohol and believe God can restore him to wholeness and sanity. I have done this by surrendering my will to the care of God.

Because alcoholism is as much a symptom as a disease, the alcoholic must face his character defects honestly. I have done this by asking God to reveal mine to me, and I pray daily for help with specific defects. I know that, unless my character and personality change, I will likely drink again.

Just over two years ago, I was so depressed I didn't want to live. I would wake up every morning not wanting to get up. I was full of dread and simply lacked interest in life. But ever since I stopped drinking, I have prayed that God would give me peace and joy every morning, and this He has done.

The Holy Spirit has taken my depression away, helped me become less self-centered and enabled me to be a channel of blessing to others, relating to them without ulterior motives or hidden agenda. And my anxieties are greatly diminished. In my prayers, I have told God that if those anxieties served a useful purpose, I would accept them and live with them. However, I've not had a severe anxiety attack since, only a few minor ones I can cope with.

Drinking problems stem from basic instincts that get out of balance: need for security, urge to reproduce, need for social belonging. Aggravated by alcohol, deadly sins—pride, anger, greed, envy, gluttony and sloth—ever act upon my basic instincts to corrupt them. The apostle Paul often referred to himself as a sinner and spoke of the constant battle within himself of the old nature against the new nature (see Rom. 7:15-25). The apostle's statement, descriptive of painful experience, is also true of me, for my old nature—though its effect is weakening—is still with me.

Romans 3:23 tells us: "For all have sinned and come short of the glory of God" (*KJV*). Sin makes us spiritually dead and drags us to hell, but thank God that, though "the wages of sin is death . . . the gift of God is eternal life through Jesus Christ our Lord" (Rom. 6:23, *KJV*).

I have peace and joy in my life today that I never had when I was excusing my sin and accommodating my life-style to alcoholism. What makes the difference now is that I am honestly facing my sin and asking God for help daily. Alcohol stunts growth mentally, physically and spiritually. Without alcohol, I am beginning to grow again in all areas, but most importantly spiritually. In these two years I've experienced more spiritual growth than in my entire previous Christian life.

"Therefore if any man be in Christ, he is a new creature: old things are passed away; behold, all things are become new" (2 Cor. 5:17, *KJV*). For me, old things are passing away, slowly but surely. No doubt it will take a lifetime. But I rejoice that new things are beginning to take place in my life.

I've returned to a very rewarding pastorate and no longer teach school. But I'm not in the ministry to boss people around through fear. Nor am I looking for status symbols or power. I simply want to help people and bring the comfort of the gospel to them.

Recently I baptized a recovering alcoholic in a pond near our church. The evening was cool, but the Spirit was warm. Tom made a public confession and gave his life to Jesus Christ. During the baptism, it showered briefly, so we all got baptized. We laughed and returned to church in a holy hush to enjoy whipped-cream cake and quiet fellowship. These are the things I enjoy in my life now.

A part of my recovery program and also part of my life now is the discipline and joy of meditation and prayer. As I live one day at a time, I'm trying to practice the Lord's command: "But seek ye first the kingdom of God, and his righteousness; and all these things shall be added unto you. Take therefore no thought for the morrow: for the morrow shall take thought for the things of itself. Sufficient unto the day is the evil thereof" (Matt. 6:33-34, *KJV*).

The psalmist speaks of this experience as a moment-by-moment walk with God (see Ps. 1 and Ps. 143:8-10). Having experienced His forgiveness, mercy and continuing grace, I am more aware now how needful it is to stay close to Him through prayer and study of the Word.

Restoration to others is still another part of the AA recovery program. The alcoholic is encouraged to list persons who have been hurt and harmed by his drinking and to make amends to them. This harm may have been physical, emotional, mental or spiritual. And much such harm is caused by neglect as by favoritism. I've begun to make such restoration and much healing has already taken place. It is an ongoing process.

Restoration of my relationship to my family has been improving, too. Soon I'll have two grandchildren. My sons are having productive careers in college and the military. Their mother and I attended their weddings and look forward to sharing important events in their lives.

I've been making amends to my children, their mother, former friends, my brother and others. Although I can't make amends to my parents, since both have now died of alcoholism, I can help other sick and suffering alcoholics because God gives me other parents, siblings and children to love and help. In this way, I can make amends to Mom and Dad for my neglect, resentment and misunderstanding.

An additional principle of AA is that the alcoholic must share with another human being his character defects in order to gain relief from guilt and remorse. Many professionals have helped me with this need: clergy, social workers, psychologists and psychiatrists. I also share almost daily with other recovering alcoholics. I'm finding a joy that comes from processing my defects openly, but with confidentiality. This is one way God works through people and agencies to help with problems of guilt and acceptance.

Of course, confession must be made to the only One who has the power to forgive. "If we confess our sins, he is faithful and just to forgive us our sins, and to cleanse us from all unrighteousness" (John 1:9, *KJV*). However, there is value in sharing with trusted persons too. "Confess your faults one to another, and pray one for another, that ye may be healed. The effectual fervent prayer of a righteous man availeth much" (James 5:16, *KJV*).

So, I share with others, and I pray to my Lord because I want to be healed from the disease of alcoholism with its accompanying sin. The drink has been gone from my life for over two years, but the alcoholic personality is still present and needs daily ministration.

The alcoholic needs to share what God has done for him, so others can experience this newness of life and power of God in their own lives. That is my motivation in telling my story here. I can keep what I have only by giving it away.

My hope is that sharing my story will help someone else who is confused by the cunning, insidious, baffling disease of alcoholism. Alcoholism denies us peace. The Lord, working through the AA program, can bring a peace we never thought possible.

Ever helpful to me is Reinhold Niebuhr's "Serenity Prayer," which I often repeat:

> God, grant me the serenity
> To accept the things I cannot change,

The courage to change the things I can;
And the wisdom to know the difference.

How Do *You* Identify?

Alcoholism. Every day, more and more families in our nation are being affected by it in one way or another. Some families are able to cope with it, some are not. Some have sought professional help or the support of friends; others struggle along on their own. Some families eventually experience victory over this horrible disease; still others know only defeat.

Church families, too, are affected by alcoholism. And when it does happen, it is a problem that is usually left up to the pastor to handle. If a member of a congregation is experiencing an addiction to alcohol, it becomes the pastor's responsibility, his duty, to deal with it. But what does the Body of Christ do when it is the pastor who has been afflicted with alcoholism? Just as the natural family can rejoice and share in the victory that a recovering alcoholic member experiences, so may the church family share in the victory of a fellow believer, be it the pastor or the parishioner.

There are a number of ways in which the members of the Church Body may share in the process of victory attained by members recovering from alcoholism. In the same manner, the Body can share in and experience one's defeat. The key to participating in a positive recovery experience lies in our attitudes, in the way we accept, view and respond to the afflicted member of the Body, whether it be a church member or the pastor.

Our own victory in this experience comes when we

share our compassion, support and Christian love for who that afflicted member really is, a co-member of the Body of Jesus Christ. On the other hand, our defeat comes as we exhibit an attitude of rejection. When the Body of Jesus Christ fails to accept a diseased human being, complete with human frailties, as an equal member of the Body, our spirit experiences as much defeat in the eyes of God as the afflicted bodies experience to the power of the addiction. It is important for each member then to become aware of those ways in which we might participate in attitude and in actual ministry in the continued recovery and victory of any brother and sister over the disease of alcoholism.

First of all, just as it is important for the recovering alcoholic to pursue a daily walk with the Lord, it is important for supporting members of the Body to join in that walk. Jesus tells us that we are to, "Seek first his kingdom and his righteousness" (Matthew 6:33). We need to remember just how difficult that is for any of us to do when we are well! How much more difficult it must be when our bodies desire that which would lead to physical and spiritual defeat.

Your very presence and support in the daily walk with another believer could make all the difference in the world. How much better, how much easier it would be to seek the Kingdom of God with another believer walking, studying, sharing life's burden along the way. The recovering alcoholic knows the importance of experiencing God's forgiveness. It is also important that we express our love and forgiveness as well, through our participation on their road to spiritual growth.

Second, since restoration to others is an integral part of an alcoholic's recovery program, allow them the opportunity to be restored to you and to your church. Sometimes this is actually harder than it seems, or at least, more difficult than it actually ought to be within the Body of Christ. Recovering alcoholics need to seek restoration, to heal certain relationships with those individuals who have been hurt, emotionally, mentally, or spiritually. But that process may never be completed if we do not allow ourselves that close personal contact with the alcoholic.

If we continue to see them as diseased, contagious and susceptible of falling immediately back into the bottle, such personal contact will never be made. Restoration is a two-way street. We need to be more than willing to meet our brother or sister halfway.

Finally, let us support in prayer ailing members of the Body. It is so easy to simply say, "I'll pray for you," and then just walk away. Pray. Really pray. Pray real words. Pray in the presence of those who need your prayers. Many of us will never know what it means to have someone hold our hand, put an arm around our shoulder and in our very presence, ask God to personally bless and touch our lives. Each one of us needs to learn that as members of the Body of Christ, church members make up our spiritual family. Our words and prayers can work for the good of others and help bring victory into our lives as well!

7

Criticism and Rejection:
A Fact of Life

It *is* a fact of life. We will receive criticism and
rejection. Even Jesus, in His perfection, experienced criticism and rejection. And this pastor
was no exception. Yet because of special knowledge and understanding he was able to deal
with conflict in his church and accept the criticism and rejection for what it really was!

When the call came to pastor Happy Valley Church, I
was living with my family in the north woods, happily and
successfully supporting them as the teaching principal of
our local elementary school. Although our life there had
been pleasant, and my family was settled and contented, I
had been experiencing an unfulfilled longing since graduat-

ing from seminary to be in the ministry. And so, the call brought me great excitement, and I looked forward to the days ahead.

But that call also brought with it a certain amount of fear—a nagging fear of failing in the ministry. Digging out my notes from Pastoral Theology, I completed a crash review in "how to do it." I didn't want to make any major mistakes.

I relearned baptizing, serving the Lord's Supper, visiting the sick, what to say and what not to say in various situations, how to counsel and how to deal with problems in the church. I was planning to follow the standard procedure of maintaining the status quo for the first year, observing, evaluating, praying, learning the job, becoming acquainted with the people, identifying problems.

When the time arrived to assume my responsibilities as pastor of Happy Valley Church, I was ready! If I followed the rules, surely success would be the result. And indeed the first year was successful. There were no major crises, attendance slowly increased and the atmosphere seemed healthy and supportive. Evidently, that Pastoral Theology course was paying off, and it looked as if we would continue into the future with smooth sailing.

The "honeymoon" lasted about 12 months, for the first rumblings of discontent began shortly after the end of our first year. Would you believe that the issue was Bible translations? Although I used the "correct" translation from the pulpit, a small, but vocal group with strong convictions on this matter, pressed for rigid controls on which translations should be used and even brought into the church building.

Although I was a novice problem solver when it came to church matters, the leaders and I approached the issue with counseling, discussion and input from all interested parties. And yet, no matter what we did to resolve the tensions, the instigators would not be satisfied. They remained adamant in their views, rejected the church and me and eventually moved on down the road where they started a new church more consistent with their convictions.

It was a painful experience for our church body and for me personally. It was also my first inkling that not all problems can be solved, and that there was some truth in the old saying, "You can't satisfy all of the people all of the time." Even though the theological differences here were somewhat minor, people were still leaving our church because of them.

Could it be that the issue at stake does not have to be major, but that the church often becomes a battleground for the unresolved personal conflicts of many of the parishioners? For example, the man who has never learned to relate properly to authority will soon chafe under the authoritative teaching of a pastor or Sunday School teacher. The woman who has had a poor and possibly damaging relationship with her father may have some difficulty relating to authority figures in the church. The individual with low self-esteem can easily strike out against fellow church members when not properly recognized or given attention.

Could it be that the pastor of a church may come under attack even though he's done nothing to deserve it, simply because of unresolved issues in the lives of his parishioners? It may be that the real issue is not a Bible translation, but something much deeper. It is for that reason that it is essential to maintain perspective, to avoid personalizing the criticism and to aim for objectivity in offering help to those individuals who may be hurting deep down inside.

It would have been nice to have had the time to think it all over. But our next church crisis was already upon us. A young man returned home from Bible school with tremendous enthusiasm for starting a bus ministry. The church should be built around the Sunday School, he thought, as he proceeded to fill our facilities with unchurched children from the area, some of whom were a bit difficult to manage. Our teaching staff was unprepared for this new ministry, and there was a sudden and urgent demand for additional staff.

Some of our church members began to talk about the need for expanded facilities in order to serve this growing ministry, but others were not so sure. And it turned out that there were some very strong feelings on both sides. I know; I got it in both ears.

One group believed that we were already making an impact on these same children through our existing youth program, and that should be sufficient because we didn't have the finances to begin a building program at that time. If the church was interested in growing, they said, let the evangelism and church growth take place as individuals and families reached out to others, drawing them to salvation and then into the church body.

But there were others who felt expansion would be a step of faith honoring to the Lord, a step that He would bless. Both sides of the issue were discussed in board meeting after board meeting. If the issue remained unsettled, any kind of ministry would come to a standstill.

Finally, it was decided that a building program at that time was not in the best interest of Happy Valley Church. But it was a decision that did not please everyone. The young man who had initiated the bus ministry left the church, taking others with him. They felt that they could no longer be a part of a church that did not have the faith to "preach the gospel to every creature" (Mark 16:15, *KJV*).

The departure of that young man and a number of his followers made me think of the truth of an old gospel hymn, "Onward Christian soldiers, marching as to war,"[1] because the fact is, we are engaged in warfare and criticism is sometimes a by-product of that warfare. We have an enemy who goes about seeking victims to devour and destroy, and Satan will even use disgruntled and discouraged members of the Body as a means to stir up trouble between fellow Christians. Satan delights in destroying the peace, harmony and growth of the Church by setting brother against brother with suspicions, jealousies and misunderstandings. Paul reminds us in Ephesians 6:10-17 that God has provided us with spiritual armor to fight Satan, but the tendency at Happy Valley Church was to put on the armor to fight one another.

I felt like *I* needed armor when our next problem arose, this time over our style of church worship. One couple departed because they felt that I should not spend any time in sermon preparation, but should simply stand up on Sunday mornings and allow the Holy Spirit to speak through me. They represented a group in our church who desired more informal and spontaneous worship. Yet, at the same time, a second couple left our church because our worship services were not formal or worshipful enough. There were so many people coming and going that it was time to put revolving doors on the front of the church. It seemed to me that it was a no-win situation. No matter which way I turned, people were leaving.

Instead of trying to deal with the rejection, I needed to deal with the issue that church hoppers are a fact of life for many evangelical churches. Instead of carrying a burden of guilt, and feeling rejected by those who were leaving, I could find some comfort in the fact that many other churches seem to face similar losses. In fact, there often seems to be a syndrome or pattern when it comes to these kinds of losses.

A couple begins to attend your church. At first, they keep to themselves, just observing from the sidelines. You get the feeling as a pastor that they are checking you out. After attending a few Sunday morning services they show up at an evening service, and you pick up on the fact that they are "old-timey" Christians—they bring well-worn Bibles, they know all of the songs without looking at the books, they seem responsive to the teaching of God's Word. And when you introduce yourself, you discover that they are from a nearby church.

After some weeks, you visit in their home and find out that their reason for attending your church is because their former church just didn't measure up. Perhaps the pastor's messages weren't biblical enough or the music was too dull or too lively. Maybe the people were unfriendly, maybe there was too much emphasis placed on giving or maybe their gifts and talents were not appreciated or used. It could be one or all of the above. But anyway, they really like your church and your preaching is "outstanding." You leave their home feeling good; your church has passed the test.

But watch out! Underneath the pleasure that you have added another tithing member is the nagging thought that in just a few months, or years, this couple will be visiting another church, talking with another pastor with a list of complaints about your church and ministry, perhaps saying the service is too formal or informal. Instead of facing the differences and making the necessary compromises that would demonstrate Christian love and loyalty, it's easier for them to hop and take their problems with them.

It was here that I reached the conclusion that no one church can meet all the varied and legitimate preferences of any one individual. Some people need openness, to "let it all hang out." Others need privacy. Some need to be demonstrative in their worship, with hands raised and verbal affirmation of the truth as it is presented. Others need and enjoy ritual and the liturgy of the church, such as the solemn celebration of the Lord's Supper.

Some come to church to hear a seminary lecture type of sermon because they approach God with their intellect, while others want to have their emotions stirred. New Christians want to hear about the grace of God, forgiveness of sin and the death, burial and resurrection of Jesus. Others feel that the whole counsel of God should be taught.

I wasn't going to let it get to me. I was beginning to understand that no one church or minister can ever hope to satisfy the personal preferences of every person who "tries out" a particular church. I reminded myself of that fact over and over again, but I continued to feel the pain of criticism and the hurt of rejection as the strengths of our church went unnoticed and its inadequacies magnified.

I was beginning to feel like an old-timer, though far from an expert, in the matter of criticism, conflict and problem solving. Each new problem brought its inevitable pain, rejection, hurt feelings, anger, sleepless nights and even tears. I may have spent time in seminary classes, but I was still learning the fact that rejection is a real part of the ministry and that there are no simplistic answers to emotionally-charged issues. To accept a call to ministry is to accept a call to face eventual withdrawal of some members from our own church family.

After 12 years at Happy Valley Church, I've just begun to deal with the fact that when it comes to ministry, rejection comes with the turf. Rejection comes on the corporate level when members reject one another, and it comes on the personal level when members reject their pastor. Whether or not I agreed with those who were dissatisfied, I became an object of anger and criticism. But it is my conviction that God intends to use our difficulties to shape and develop our characters. Even in rejection, there are lessons of great benefit to learn if we remain teachable.

When it comes to dealing with some of the rejection I have faced, I have found great solace and strength in the Gospel of Mark as the writer demonstrates opposite reactions to Jesus and His ministry. He was embraced by some, rejected by others, and all of this in spite of His sinless perfection. Gentle when necessary and firm when the situation required it, Jesus was above reproach in every area of His life. And yet, in spite of His perfection, Jesus experienced rejection.

At first this rejection was by just a few, but it became progressively more intense. By the end of His ministry, Jesus was rejected by all but a few faithful followers. Those of us who have been called to minister need to ask ourselves the questions: Is the disciple above his master? Are we above rejection?

Yes, 12 years have come and gone. Today the Happy Valley Church is prospering under God's good hand of blessing. We have experienced our share of rejection, criticism and church hopping, but all of that seems to be behind us now. The future is as bright as this beautiful spring day. It's nice to have arrived!

Oh, by the way, one of our church leaders just called. He feels that the constitution adopted by the church at my request is inadequate. And my wife reminded me the other day that Mrs. Filled-with-the-Spirit has not been to church in three weeks, and the new couple from the church across town has suggested that I wear a blue robe in the pulpit like Dr. Schuller wears on TV as it would improve the quality and dignity of our services.

Oh, well, here we go again!

How Do *You* Identify?

Is it really true that since the Church is made up of people, there will always be those who will criticize and reject those who are not carbon copies of themselves? If so, is there any real hope for peace within the Body of Christ?

It seems like it would be so easy to place all of the blame for such actions and attitudes on that old culprit, human nature. It almost gives us an excuse to remind the pastor that last Sunday's sermon was just a bit too long, and that the tenors were more than a little off-key. Where or when will it ever end?

Believe it or not, criticism and rejection are present in every church. Life in the Church and pastoral ministry should not be a day-by-day struggle to survive the barbs and flaming arrows of criticism leveled by little old ladies who feel there is too much of a beat to the second hymn, or by deacons who feel that the pastor's wife wears just a tad too much make-up. But that's what happens. Maybe we need to become more aware of how to effectively deal with this kind of attitude before it gets started.

We may not set out to be overly critical, but we do have two ears, which often act as funnels to fill our minds with ammunition. So much of our own critical spirit finds its roots in the opinions and feelings of others as their hostile words, complaints and ideas turn our heads. Believers need to guard against voicing what are not really their own heartfelt concerns, but rather the warmed-over tirades of family members, friends and neighbors.

Someone once found this prayer written on a sheet of paper and carried in the purse of his godly mother:

> God teach me not to listen to
> "They say" and "I have heard",
> Let me not injure anyone
> By idly spoken words.
> God teach me blamelessly to live,
> And generously too,
> And help me always to be fair,
> And tolerant, and true.

The next time we are prepared to give voice to criticism, we might do well to stop for a moment and ask, Is what we have to say really how we truly feel, or is it something that we heard complained about at the dinner table last week? Will our criticism serve to make the Body of Christ stronger or will it add to present unrest and fuel the critical spirit of the one who gave birth to the opinion in the first place?

As long as human beings make up the Church, the Body of Jesus Christ, it will never be perfect. As long as the Church has been in existence there has been criticism, and there will continue to be. But that is no reason for any one of us to give up on the Body. We may not be perfect, but there is hope that we might become "perfected"!

The Body might not be perfect, but the Head of the Body is perfect. As we strive to become more like Him each day, there is hope for the future of the Church, and perhaps one day the spirit of criticism and rejection will be laid to rest.

8

God's Love Endures All Things

Only by God's grace and through His unconditional love is this pastor able to live and cope
with the horrible truth that relentlessly looms
its head to destroy his life and his family. Diag-
nosis: His wife is manic depressive. Prognosis:
The episodes will return along with all their
awful memories and recurrent themes. But,
God's love endures all things.

It was all happening again. But, somehow I still
couldn't believe it. I was stunned, paralyzed, just like
always.

I don't know why I can't seem to handle this. I'm
known as a man of action, decisiveness. Plans of action are
usually immediate and clear. Except when this happens.

This was the fifth time in 15 years of marriage, but this

time it would prove to be extremely severe and painful. Penny wakened me at 6:30 A.M., Monday, June 8, 1980.

"Craig," I groggily heard, "I'm leaving you. I'm going to live with Richard Smart."

"Penny, wait!" Leaping from bed I followed her down the stairs. Was this a bad dream? No, it was harsh reality. I was wide awake now, "Penny . . . " I tried to reason with my wife once again. I'd been through scenarios like this before.

"I've made up my mind. The kids are with friends. We're no good for each other. We should have never gotten married. I'm not happy. I'm going shopping with Kathy and I'll pick up my stuff in a few days. I talked it all over with Reg [a mutual friend] all night. He agrees. Bye."

With that she was out the door, in her car and gone.

For the next hour I was riveted to the kitchen floor. It felt as if I was dying—the memories of the past 15 years flashed through my mind as the pain gushed out of me in great sobs and groanings. I lived the next 16 days it seemed in slow motion, even though events occurred with amazing speed.

I am a minister in an evangelical denomination known as a bastion of conservatism in theology and life. My particular congregation was denominationally known for its traditionalism, uniquely so in areas of family and marriage. In church politics, my board were heavy hitters, historically big on image and low on compassion and understanding.

"Penny, you can't do this to me, to us, to the kids! They'll force me to resign!" I yelled to the earless walls of the expansive, four-bedroom colonial church manse! But she did!

A host of emotion-riddled thoughts raced through my

mind: disbelief, anger, resentment, hurt, loss, despair, helplessness. *Calm down,* I tried to tell myself. *You've been through this all before with Penny. This isn't the first time. You've heard this all before.*

And I had. But my congregation hadn't, and everything Penny said and did in the next couple of weeks was for the most part conducted among the more gullible and, unfortunately, was half-believed by many in the congregation. The dividing line between emotional stability and instability is very narrow. The damage that was done by words, half-believing ears and eyes, and by Penny's outlandish behavior, goals and stories were almost insurmountable for a community of Christians and for me. Indeed, the truth shall set us free, but rarely is untruth clearly untrue.

Penny has been diagnosed as having a "bipolar affective disorder," more popularly known as manic/depression, with apparently organic roots, i.e. it has a biological base and is affected by one's environment. It all began to surface 16 years ago, a few months after we were married; we were both 20 years old. We had both been raised in very sheltered families and churches. Emotional illness was little understood. Primarily it was considered to result from some gross sin or because of a serious flaw in one's character, morals and faith. One of Penny's many sisters still believes that Penny has no illness at all, but that Penny's problems are wholly brought on by my domineering ways and personality, which God allows and, indeed, actively wills, because either Penny, myself or both have horribly sinned in the past or are willing agents of Satan in the present.

In 1980, many of our acquaintances still harbored that kind of theory in order to explain what they were observing. Prior to 1980, Penny was institutionalized four times. Since then, she has been hospitalized twice for the same illness. No matter how many doctors have diagnosed Penny's difficulties as being a "bipolar affective disorder" with organic roots, many of our friends, acquaintances and congregations largely believe that Penny, myself or both have serious moral flaws in our character, or that we simply don't know how to live and behave as married Christians ought to. Many of Penny's family cannot accept that her illness has organic roots because maybe those "roots" are also in their genes, and this might make their parents more culpable.

From 1965 to 1970, I lived with the belief—often reinforced by Penny herself during her manic episodes—that my personality and goals were largely responsible for her depression and/or mania. Doctors, too, reinforced that belief to some degree by their silence and methods of treatment. I was told that I was too insensitive; we spent weeks in therapy so I could learn to become more sensitive. I was told that I operated far too much on an intellectual level while Penny lived mostly on an emotional level; we spent more months in therapy so I could learn to be more emotional. I was told that I was egocentric in pursuing my life's goals of being called to the ministry which were thought to be too demanding for Penny; it was recommended that I should allow her to attain some of her personal goals. I took a year's leave of absence from seminary studies. In my denomination, seminary is normally a four-year postcollege program; it took me five and a half years. During this time, Penny entered a trade school to pursue her career goals. She also wanted to become pregnant. Penny always wanted at least six children.

Around the time of each hospitalization, there were

several recurring themes. One of those now-familiar themes related to divorce. Penny insisted she wanted one each time. She would telephone everybody we knew without regard for the time of day or night. Then, she would repeat every intimate detail of our marriage and everything I might have said that was hurtful. We finally adopted children, and when she began a manic episode, she'd threaten to have them returned to the adoption agency. I would hear a familiar refrain: "I don't love you anymore. You don't satisfy my needs and never have." Preceding her hospitalizations there often would be big spending sprees, sexual promiscuity, hallucinatory episodes, grandiose goals, vulgar and profane speech.

Her family—six brothers and six sisters—for the most part held me responsible for inducing these actions and reducing their sister to such a person. My father claimed that if Penny would just stop taking all those birth-control pills, everything would be fine.

Family and a Christian community of friends are important, but sometimes in the face of such abnormality, family, friends and the Christian community can make matters much worse through their involvement as they postulate a thousand half-baked notions. I have come to understand that for many this might be necessary to protect some order in their own lives. But until the 1970 hospitalization—Penny's third since we were married, were it not for the grace of God, dogged determination and a few special professors, I believe I would have given up on life, certainly on God!

During her 1970/71 hospitalization, after two grueling weeks when it seemed to me that this time Penny would not stop her manic behavior, one of the doctors on her team called me into his office. Penny, he explained, was finally diagnosed as having manic/depressive illness.

I had never heard of it! "Do you mean," I exploded, "that I'm not to blame for all this!"

He hedged a little. He went on to explain that the "experts" were unsure whether this type of mental illness was genetically caused or merely predisposed and thus triggered by environmental stress.

Great, I remember thinking. *What does that mean?*

He didn't want to talk much more about Penny's newly diagnosed illness. Psychiatrists never want to talk to spouses. They feel safer hiding behind the age-old cloak of "confidentiality." With all the pent-up anger, resentment, hurt and pain heaped on me from without and accepted from within for the past four years, I blurted out: "But what about *my* feelings? What about all *I've* been told that *I've* been doing wrong for Penny? What about *my* right and need to know what's going on here?" He calmly and quietly recommended another psychiatrist for me to see!

What he wanted from me was the legal right to administer to Penny a new experimental drug called "lithium." He analogously explained that lithium is to manic/depression what insulin is to diabetes. Penny would be placed on the drug for six months and then removed from it, as it was only experimental and could severely damage her kidneys. It might also have other adverse side effects such as: weight gain, lethargy, possible toxicity and low sexual drive, to name a few.

Stunned, I said, "Yeah, go ahead."

Penny has never really forgiven me or accepted lithium very well. She has always detested taking any medication for anything, including aspirin. To this day Penny believes that she really doesn't need lithium; that I have always forced her into her hospitalizations as a means to control her life, all of which is partially reinforced by members of her family, some of the Christian community and not a few past friends.

Surprisingly, lithium seemed to work quite well, and Penny didn't experience the projected side effects, at least in those beginning years of usage. Our marriage radically improved in all facets, so it seemed. I returned to seminary. Penny seemed really happy. I graduated and entered an internship prior to ordination in a very large congregation. Things were indeed looking up! Even after Penny went off lithium as prescribed, nothing adverse seemed to happen. But the fallen world in which we live has a way of sneaking up on us.

Penny continued to want a child. After several tests for Penny and myself, it was determined that I am incurably sterile. Penny claims to this day that it was only because I didn't try hard enough, that I didn't want her to have anything good like a baby of her own, that I hurried her off to an adoption agency instead of allowing her to be artificially inseminated.

It was then that the evil one turned the screw a little tighter. The senior pastor where I was an intern called me into his office about four months before my ordination. Penny, he compassionately tried to tell me, was having an affair with a black man, 22 years older than she. The affair had been going on for the past two years and Penny was livid that I was so insensitive and too stupid to notice it for this long a time. "She really wants you to know," he painfully went on. "That's why she told me and that's why I'm telling you."

A new theme emerged in Penny's illness. And that was why, on June 8, 1980, the man's name and Penny's deranged plans reopened some very deep wounds. *Will I never be free from this horror,* I wept alone in the stillness of that big house. *Why, God? What have I done? What shall I do now? Can I, will we ever recover? No one will believe me that it's mainly an illness! They'll all believe the father of lies through Penny's irrational mind!*

It has always amazed me why people find irrationality so believable. Is it because what we do not understand we'd rather not confront? Does it have something to do with preconceived notions about mental illness, divorce and anger as being "sinful" and therefore something "good" Christians should not struggle with? Is it because we so easily accept that which goes on all about us in the world, but we don't expect to have these kinds of problems surface among Christians? And when they do—especially in the lives of your pastor and his wife—would we rather retreat into safe disbelief instead of deal with the ugly reality?

Penny did leave just as she said, coming back only long enough to threaten that she would return for the children—our four-year-old son and our six-month-old daughter. "We're not fit to care for them," she angrily taunted me, "their birth parents would do a better job of parenting." Then, abruptly, she faced me with a demonic look in her eyes, "I'll do things to you and make you suffer like you've made me suffer—you'll be jobless and penniless." She partly succeeded.

For the next two weeks, I rarely knew exactly where Penny was. I knew she was in a large midwestern city. Our denominational headquarters were located there. She drove her dilapidated car, charging a host of repairs and fuel, motel bills (she lived almost the entire time in motels), food, clothes and entertainment. She put everything on credit cards or just left the establishment, forgetting to sign the charge slip. I spent many hours with a variety of motel owners, telling them I had cancelled that particular card. (I had to do something to curtail the thousands of dollars being charged.) Penny went from doctor to doctor on her own, but found no relief from the driving mania inside her—she wasn't hearing them say what her manic self wanted to hear.

She tried to purchase a home by pawning her jewelry, and almost succeeded. She kept two reporters of the city's largest newspaper busy for several hours with a juicy story about one of our denomination's ministers, until it dawned on them that something was radically wrong. Penny is an adept storyteller. During her manic phases, she's peculiarly equipped to gain the sympathy of pastors who have a great need to be helpful to distressful souls imploring their help through half-believable, but fabricated stories. Penny told them that she was a victim of wife-abuse and that her husband was a minister of the gospel, no less. She was looking the role, too: harried, sleepless, traumatized eyes—she had left her contacts in for too many days and now couldn't get them out—and all this inside a body that for almost three weeks now had been in constant motion. She busied her friends with hallucination-filled evenings of the FBI and CIA out to "get" her, with me leading the charge. Her "lover" pleadingly called me to put her in a hospital, recounting several lurid tales.

I filed for divorce to protect the kids from being taken by Penny on her wild escapades. Although I had always intended to rip up these papers after Penny became well, this was another incident Penny found virtually impossible to understand, forgive or forget.

Finally, at the urging of several people, I drove to the

city where she had fled and tried to find her. Inevitably, when Penny begins her manic phase and spins her tales of woe, literally hundreds of people get embroiled in the scenario because, as a minister who had served three congregations by this time, we knew hundreds of people. For the first couple of hours, she appears very believable to them. Then they realize she's very distraught, and finally within a few days they're begging me to do something, because they know they've been manipulated into becoming my accusers and Penny's rescuers, both roles which they suddenly no longer wish to play. Well-meaning friends often are placed into incredibly difficult situations. If they could have remained at least neutral, they would have helped Penny return to some semblance of order. By becoming involved in the scenario, they now became part of the ongoing problem.

When I finally found Penny, an army recruiter was signing her up with the army. She was scheduled for her physical three days later. She never made it.

That afternoon I physically carried her, kicking and screaming, into the car while someone else drove. We took her to a Christian hospital for emotional illness, the same hospital she had been in four times previously. When she got there, she voluntarily admitted herself.

During the next two weeks, the hospital called twice to say that I had to be ready to appear in court in order to restrain her for treatment. It never came to that; each time I was about to leave home for court, Penny relented and volunteered to remain in the hospital until her doctors would give her a medical release. Yet, from June 24 to July 6, when I tried to visit Penny, she would often taunt me and pathetically cry with fists clenched, "I'm going to kill you for putting me here and for trying to take away my children!" Then immediately she would switch and moan, "Why don't you take a gun and kill me instead?"

Meanwhile, I was, of course, not in my congregation's pulpit or at my office tending my "flock" in any way. Politically, I did have problems in the church. Half my board and many in the congregation were screaming for my resignation. These people reasoned that, if Penny was only half right in her charges, I should be dismissed from the ministry. If Penny were totally wrong, I still should be dismissed, for how could I be a pastor and leader of God's people when I obviously could not "manage my own household well", a qualification urged upon Timothy by Paul as a condition of church leadership (see 1 Tim. 3:5).

More than this, I wondered how in the world I could continue as a minister of the gospel with my credibility so terribly damaged. It didn't matter at this moment where the truth lay, the fact and reality were that in people's perceptions "where there was smoke, there was fire." Maybe I wasn't largely responsible for what was occurring in Penny's life, but then again maybe I was, even just a little, they reasoned. I more than half believed it myself at the time. Maybe God was trying to tell me that I had misheard His calling. Maybe I truly was an emotionless person. When it comes to patience and understanding with others, I am not always perfect. Maybe I was seriously, emotionally flawed, and was bringing all this pain on Penny. And, even if this was only a little bit true, wasn't our family far too scarred for me to continue shepherding God's people? True, pastors and their families are far from perfect, but shouldn't they have their acts together just a little more than their congregation, in order to lead and be an example? All these questions and more pounded away in my mind and ears for many, many weeks. I knew the enemy within and his power to destroy.

On July 15, 1980, something remarkable happened to add to a remarkable past few weeks: Penny telephoned me, "I want to talk to you with my doctor." Then ensued several discussions, breathing a quality of air I had never before breathed since Penny's illness manifested itself. Her therapist, a beautiful Church of the Nazarene minister, explained to the two of us the whys, wherefores and how-comes of her illness.

"Penny, tell him he's not primarily responsible for all that's happened these past few weeks. And be honest." I can still hear him say this as a fountain of tears flooded forth from the depths of my being. For Penny, it was extremely painful. It is one thing to be *the* participant during all the irrationality and despicable, obnoxious behavior that accompanies acute mania, or even delirious mania. It is wholly another thing to accept responsibility, even partial responsibility for the beast, on a conscious level, knowing that the beast can't be controlled even when you want to with all your might.

Penny was owning up to her responsibility because she loved me deeply, as well as her children, and she wanted us to love her more. All the awful business of sexual promiscuity, deranged lies, threats of divorce, etc., were simply manifestations of an inner being thrown into chaos by a genetically deranged, chemical imbalance. True, our personalities interact along with the particular environment within which we roam together, and we thus participate, sometimes trigger, and surely overreact to this uncontrolled and unwanted imbalance. But, it was not because of a woeful lack of faith—belief in Jesus Christ—or because

God was seeking to punish either Penny or me as though we were some awful sinners.

The bipolar affective disorder is variously described by a variety of specialists and experts in the field. The problem is that these experts themselves do not, and cannot, precisely define the illness, pinpoint the causes or even satisfactorily prescribe a treatment for cure or even prevention. No one really knows precisely how lithium works, or if it triggers mania at various times or even what are the totality of its possible, future side effects. It works in a large number of cases or at least tends to ameliorate and restrain both mania and the depression side.

Generally, mania is described as significant elevation in mood and activity, utmost confidence and invincibility, capable of undertaking any task. Usually, it displays a high degree of energy, grandiose schemes, spending and gambling sprees, even extra-marital affairs and sexual promiscuity, although the thought processes are actually quite shallow. Mania usually has with it a steady stream of consciousness or flight of ideas. The person often bolts from his usual surroundings and takes on quite different life goals and perspectives, is usually poorly articulated and not well-reasoned. If the person feels interfered with in any way, he can become quite abusive, angry and obnoxious.

What's terribly important to realize is that each person with the illness follows a unique script. Further, not all people who exhibit similarities to the above description are the least bit manic. And then there's the depression side, which almost no one sees but the spouse and family. Yet it's inevitably there, following and preceding the manic phases, often equalling the severity of the mania, but in the opposite direction. While people around the manic often feel the intensity and brunt of the episode, the depression side is totally experienced by the person alone.

Some experts believe that mania is simply the over manifestation of the depths of the internally felt pain and the hopeless, helpless, overwhelming, uncontrollable, tormented feelings. Most doctors, now, prescribe a variety of drugs including lithium, antipsychotics and antidepressants along with ongoing psychotherapy to cope with the illness. Many with the illness, perhaps even most, never become embroiled in the depth of scenario experienced by Penny in her mania.

It's of paramount importance for those around manic-depressives to remember at all times that they do not want the behavior so often associated with the mania. It isn't their lack of genuine Christian faith. It isn't because they are deficient in morals, character, affection, commitment and loyalty. They are not "sickees."

During most of the time when the disease is dormant, Penny is a wonderfully loving, compassionate, understanding, patient, caring and deeply spiritual person. Consider the guilt and shame that overwhelms her and others like her, when one of these episodes subsides and she desperately wants to return to her former goals and commitments in life. Add, too, the pain she experiences, half-consciously watching her own personality and perspective radically changing, only to face later the painful and long road of reversal, which inevitably follows.

Who really can explain, much less feel, those awful "black hole" feelings of utter despair amid the darkness of depression. While mania is filled with obnoxious behavior, depression is often almost behaviorless in expression. It may be much easier to accept and deal with for others, but it is far more damning internally than mania. And, there is little to stop depression from happening; it inevitably follows a manic phase.

Penny, for instance, is a highly intelligent and vivacious woman, deeply in love with life, her husband, her family and people around her. Yet she knows the pain she's caused and the damage done to those relationships she holds most dear. She knows that most, if not all of us, tend to remember unendingly those things of the past that are extremely vivid. She knows also that some things cannot be undone, only hopefully forgiven and in time forgotten. And she knows, as we all do, that try as we may to prevent them, the episodes will return along with all their awful memories and recurrent themes.

Only two things are certain and allow us to continue with a zest for life: (1) the impact of the grace of God: "Jesus loves us! This we know, for the Bible tells us so"; and (2) our love for each other, for better for worse, in the redeeming Christ, whose love outlasts all else.

Too often, far too often, I, like others, have seen and remember only Penny, the manic/depressive, instead of Penny the beautiful Christian woman in whom God is deeply working. Who else could keep her going with love and compassion and faith and hope throughout a life like she's had? No! Penny is not some pathetic, helpless, hopeless, faithless, immoral lout! She is instead a woman of deep faith, endurance, resilience and love for Christ and His Kingdom. What other explanation could there be to account for her continued faith in God and desire to live and work and love in His world?

We have often accorded sainthood in the annals of history on those who have endured great hardship and have still kept the faith. Are not Penny and the many like her in other situations and places examples of such saints of

God? *O God, how I love this woman and the God in whose image she's created!*

How Do *You* Identify?

There are a number of things to be learned from the experience of this chapter, which may be helpful to the Body of Christ when it comes to ministering to other members who may be dealing with similar trauma in their lives.

First of all, it is extremely important for the Christian community to remember and believe that what God has declared to be "clean" in Jesus Christ, we ought not to declare as "unclean" (see Acts 10:15). In the final analysis, it really doesn't matter if it is a disease that causes the total breakdown of a marriage and surrounding relationships or whether it is the human deficiencies of that relationship which trigger a latent illness. It doesn't matter, because the painful effects are the same. In that light, it is important that members of the Body do not attempt to visualize all that might be wrong in such a relationship or analyze in detail what each part has done wrong.

What we must see is the irresistible, overwhelming grace of God at work in a relationship where love exists. Could mere, natural human love supercede major obstacles within the pervasive environment of our current American, marital perspectives? Christians today need to look at the trials of their lives and see the love and grace of God which leads them through the victory.

Second, pastors and lay members of the Body need to deal with a peculiar tendency to want to rescue every hurting soul as if they were the Mediator, Himself. In so doing, many of us find ourselves embroiled in situations and circumstances that we are wholly incapable of resolving, thereby often making matters worse. It may be better if we were to readily acknowledge that in some circumstances an unbeliever who knows his profession can, and often does, become a mightier instrument in the hand of God than a well-meaning believer who is ignorant of the maladies of the human personality.

There are times when Christians must realize that there are events and situations which occur in a fallen world that defy all explanation, and for us to try to offer solutions and opinions without understanding may only intensify the problem. Just because we serve a rational God who created an orderly and rational universe does not mean that, in a fallen world, all things (or even most things) can be explained, rationalized or be understood to have a specific, known cause.

Third, it is important that we avoid the inescapable tendency to give up. Countless numbers of people, Christian people, have urged the couple we have just read about to divorce and for the pastor to quit the ministry. The stream of questions is endless. But this is what faith is all about. It is not walking by sight. It is hearing and believing the Word more clearly and deeply than the noises of evil and drawing on the strength of our Lord.

A fourth point deals with reality and the Church today. Not all congregations will be able to respond, accept and live with a pastor and his wife like this couple. But we need to remember that there are huge numbers of hurting people and troubled marriages and as one member of this pastor's congregation expresses, "You know better than most the pain that we feel." All marriages have ups and downs.

And Christians are peculiarly susceptible to this kind of destruction, because too often we simplistically believe and expect that mere mental assent to the gospel will prevent all ills. Rather, true faith only helps us endure and sometimes conquer our problems.

God never desires for His children to experience pain, suffering, turmoil, chaos or death. But He does promise that those who believe in Him shall endure the dark night through His Son, Jesus Christ. Life, peace, hope, endurance, steadfastness, faith and love are all of God. It is only in the redemptive love of God that we begin to learn that difference and become better people despite the pain and in the midst of chaos.

Why people experience what they do will remain to some degree inexplicable for the moment. If we become better people, it is only because of the impact of grace in our lives in spite of the darkness. In this realization lies the power, the glory and the hope to face a new tomorrow, "Christ in you, the hope of glory" (Col. 1:27).

9

You're Great!

Do you have a positive self-image? If so, great! You'll enjoy this bit of positive reinforcement. If not, perhaps you'll feel differently when you've read how one pastor's "declaration of greatness" has changed the lives of many, beginning with his very own.

I'm great!
I'm so great, that it takes a person as great as I
    am to appreciate how great I am!
What? You think I'm great too?!
That means that you're great, because you can
    appreciate how great I am!

It's funny that the above "declaration of greatness" should surface several times in my recent years to encourage and transform crushed spirits significantly. Mine was first.

It all began with my friend Sandy making his declaration of greatness. I, of course, fully agreed and, in my agreement, was pronounced great by his declared standard. All was rather tongue-in-cheek, mind you, but still it felt good. Some inner transformation was beginning, and an outward smile grew as I went on my way laughing and declaring: "I'm great! I'm so great, that it takes a person as great as I am to appreciate how great I am!"

As I said, the declaration of greatness surfaced several times in recent years. I will tell you first of my struggle with the declaration and then of some conclusions. Then I will do the same concerning two other friends, Bill and Dave. Keep reading. You may conclude with a grin, declaring, "I'm great! I'm so great that . . . . "

The declaration with which we are dealing is so powerful because human hurt is so deep. What kind of human hurt? A dented self-image. The kind of self-image that says, "I'm worthless," "I can't do anything right" or "The world would be better off without me." Each of us with sensitivities and specific areas of weakness gets dented. Sometimes people want to hurt us deliberately, and other times we just get hurt because of our sensitivities.

Members of my family used to call me "Fats." I was a chubby kid and sensitive about it, so I got dented. I was not especially athletic. I could not play any ball sport. I never got chosen for teams, and soon I got the impression that nobody liked me. I got dented. Academically, my performance was about average and sometimes just plain weak. Tutors had to help me in algebra and Spanish; I got dented. Now those are three major areas in which a boy is evaluated—looks, sports and academics.

By the time I reached high school, my self-image was off the bottom of the chart. Without exaggeration, I would have to watch a person for a whole year before I would dare to say "Hello." And, if they did not say "Hello" in return, I would die emotionally. I would register it as another rejection. Only if I was quite sure of a friendly response could I risk the simple greeting. I was hurting.

My human hurt was not all that obvious. I could hide it and still be the life of the party. On the plus side, I was pretty good at Ping-Pong and outdoor sports. The prettiest girl in the class actually wanted me to ask her out. So my public image was fine, but I hurt privately in my self-image.

Christ began to deal with me and I began to deal with Him in these areas of need. I began to pray about my love towards others. Knowing that I had to show the love of Christ to others, I began to risk saying "Hello" to people I had known only for six months, and then three months, and then one month and finally to strangers.

Do you know what? They all said "Hello" back to me. The healing was really under way. Rather than rejection, I found acceptance.

We have all taken dents in our self-image. So when we are confronted with a wide-open acceptance, it is always healing. When my friend Sandy said, "I'm great," I could laugh and agree that he is great. In the very agreement, he then declared, "You're great," and obviously there is no arguing the decision of a great person.

Sandy, in a simple declaration, worked to heal many years of self-depreciation in his words, "You're great!" I somehow believed him because of his love for me and his openness to me. I was able to accept his encouragement. After all, when a person declares someone else to be great, it must be so!

Where does self-image come from? There are three sources from which we draw our self-evaluation: God, self and others. All are filtered through our own perspective, of course, yet some distinction exists.

Each person has some picture of God and God's attitude toward himself. It may be a lopsided picture, in which God is severely displeased and rejecting, or one in which He is totally accepting—including sinful behavior. Any such lopsided picture will be to the disadvantage of the individual in that such a picture is not real. Only the real or true attitude of God will be helpful.

The true attitude of God has room for human failure and the weaknesses of an individual without diminishing the human value as the creation of God, in His image. Also, the human potential to become sons of God in Jesus Christ adds greatly to the value of every person in the sight of God. Regardless of how a person thinks God feels about him, that impression is a significant part of his own self-image.

Self is the second source of self-image. Here, we compare and contrast ourselves with others in a number of categories. How do we rate comparatively in looks, relating, education, skills, sports, clothing, friends and so on? On a scale of 1 to 10, are we a 10? Or a 2? Again, caution is needed because we may be more severe on ourselves that we would be on others.

Also, it is possible to pad the score against ourselves by making comparisons where we are especially weak or strong. It is perhaps wiser to look at ourselves and minimize comparison. In other words, "What are my personal strengths? Are they in significant areas?" This personal evaluation is a part of self-image.

Other people are the third source of self-image. "What

do others think of me?" I receive input from every public area of life including family, employment, friendship, social situations and areas of responsibility. Everyone has an opinion of me, and what I believe they think of me contributes to my overall self-image.

So my total self-image originates in God, self and others and yet it is easily slanted because in the end, the input comes through my own filters. In my own case, when my self-image was doing so poorly, every bit of encouragement was important. When Sandy said, "You're great!" it was as if God had spoken to me. It was a gift from a friend and I accepted what he offered. It was a gift from a "great" person and that, in itself, compounded the encouragement.

A further dimension in God's healing of dented persons is that He uses dented persons to help others who have been dented. But it's not at all like the blind leading the blind. It is, rather, the healed blind man leading other blind men to healing. I had been deeply hurt when it came to my own self-image, but God had brought about healing. Now, God can use my past experiences and hurts. Through those hurts, I can better understand the fat kid who's hurting, the poor athlete and the struggling student.

What was once an area of hurting and pain is now a blessing because God has healed my self-image. In addition, He has gifted me spiritually to encourage others. Just as Sandy said it to me, I am saying it to others, "You're great!" I am reinforcing their value in the eyes of God and to me personally. I am affirming the image of God in His creation and the potential in every person to become sons of God in Jesus Christ.

Now let me tell you about Bill. We studied together in seminary and we became close friends. He was a blind man led greatly by God, possessing a dynamic personality and a brilliant mind. We ran together mornings and prayed. When we graduated, Bill and I were called to pastorates in different states. Bill went to a small rural town where he loved the people. He really invested his life in theirs. And yet, possibly because of his handicap or whatever else, the church rejected him. They had a "giant" among them and yet they were rejecting him! I couldn't believe it.

Letters came every six months or so, and over the years the rejection was becoming harder and harder for Bill to bear. I went to visit him and his family. They poured out their pain, and I hurt with them. When I heard the story and had shown my understanding, I went to battle.

I said,

> I'm great!
> I'm so great, that it takes a person as great as
> I am to appreciate how great I am.

And Bill agreed, "You are great!"
I continued,

> What? You think I'm great too!
> That means that *you're* great, because you can
> appreciate how great I am!

We all burst into laughter as Bill reaffirmed, "I *am* great!"

And his wife said to him, "You *are* great!"

"We're *all* great!" we all declared!

You see, I simply believed it, and I was not going to let some small-minded people crush the spirit out of this dear friend of mine. Months later, I received letters declaring,

"We're great!" and even years later, we still recall that important day of encouragement.

Hurting others is so cruel and senseless. Why do we pick on people in their weaknesses and emphasize their faults. Why not be as generous with others as we hope they will be with us? We know the Golden Rule, "Do unto others as you would have them do unto you" (see Matt. 7:12). Why diminish the glory of God in His creation?

If you began listing my weaknesses and spelling them out to me, it could be greatly debilitating. For instance, I'm lousy when it comes to details, and that can be tough for a pastor. I'm so single-minded that I can't think about two things at once and get anything done. So, there are a lot of things that just never get done.

But I also have strengths! If I can major on my strengths, and really "go for it" with some encouragement, I can be unstoppable! I have a drive that doesn't quit. I can set short-range goals and get there on schedule. I am even strengthening some former areas of weakness. A proper emphasis on strengths and some personal encouragement are all I need.

Then there's Dave. Dave served as a pastor until he sensed failure; not total failure, but enough to say, "Goodbye" to pastoral leadership in the Church. There was a lot of soul-searching and discouragement. His smile was not as frequent or as free as in earlier years. He was not sure of himself either. But I was. Dave *is* a great man of God. I knew it!

I had to say to him, "Dave,"

I'm *great!*
I'm *so* great, that it takes a person as great as I am to appreciate how great I am!

> What? *You* think I'm great too?!
> That means that *you're* great, because you can
>   appreciate how great I am!

It happened again. The declaration took a deep hold this time on Dave. It encouraged him. It reminded him of God's love and acceptance as His own child. We still laugh together and share the declaration of greatness and draw some real healing from it.

Note the progression. God used Sandy, a Christian layman, to significantly encourage three pastors. Pastors seem so open to dents in their self-image; their weaknesses are on public display. Their job performance will always seem to fall short of the great task of ministry. Some of them were well-dented before their ministry years. It is amazing that God calls and uses such people in ministry.

God has certainly used me in encouraging others, and yet, I am still full of dents myself. Even in the time of my greatest success, there are horrible displays of weakness. They hurt so much. I wish they would somehow go away. They just pop out publicly, right out in front, like a big red pimple on my nose.

So, my struggle continues. Basically, I have a very strong self-image right now, but it still comes under attack. Comparisons offer one form of attack. When I am talking with a very handsome man or a beautiful woman and I sense they are not interested in me, I am attacked. When I am with a pastor my age who seems to have accomplished far more in ministry than I have, I am attacked. When I am doing great in ministry, but my wife reminds me of family needs, I am attacked. Comparisons really hurt. They may not be an appropriate way to evaluate myself, but they are hard to avoid. Comparisons tend to be made against the strengths of others, and that is unfair. When there are 10 good strengths arrayed against your one, you will always lose.

Depression is another source of attack. Two days ago, your dear friend died. Yesterday, you failed to get all four of the goals for the day done, and you made one worse. Today is rainy, and the car died. The attack begins as you walk in circles in your office. Is all your work worth it? You can't get anything done. You bungle things all the time. You can't do anything right. What will you do? Where will you go from here? Self-evaluation in the middle of depression is always slanted toward the negative. You lose!

Attack from others really takes the wind out of your sails. Someone teases you too much about an area of your weakness. The church board calls in the pastor to pressure him to change in some way. A friend—at least you thought he was your friend—just nailed you in a very unkind way. The attack on your self-image came out of nowhere; you were feeling great, but now the battle is on.

Comparison, depression and criticism are all a normal part of life. They can be hurtful, but hopefully their effect can be minimized through evaluation. The bottom line is still our standing before God, and the gospel is still good news.

I am created in the image of God. This gives my life a wonderful dignity. God considers me worth His time and attention. I carry some likeness to God Himself. He individually fashioned me in my mother's womb for His own purpose (see Ps. 139:13). Although that image was marred by my sin, it was partially restored by the Spirit who renewed me in my acceptance of Christ's forgiveness. In the heavenly Kingdom I will be fully made anew in

His image! My self-image must be considered as God's image and should not be depreciated.

God can show His power in our weaknesses (see Cor. 12:9), which teaches us about humility. If a man were filled with a great sense of pride, he would be cast down by God and rejected for his failure to place God in that high place of honor. We must always sense our weakness and unworthiness before Him. Only then will we remember to call on God for forgiveness and assistance as we worship and serve Him. "God, give me enough weaknesses to remain humble before you." Our weakness is also necessary for the display of His greatness.

In my standing before God, His love is a central point of the good news. As the Bible says, "If God is for us, who can be against us?" (Rom 8:31). God loves us. What other opinion really matters? When others love us, they reflect the truth. When others hate us, they are in error, for God is truth and God is love.

We have no right to hate others, for that opposes God. We are commanded, rather, to love one another, for God is love (see 1 John 4:7,8). The same must apply to self. We must love ourselves because God loves us. God's love extends to me, even when I disregard Him. He died for me, even when I fail Him. So, I am never outside of His love!

The truth is: God deliberately created us in His image and He loves us. We have weaknesses in the light of which He shines much brighter. He displays His glory in our weakness, not using our weakness against us, but for Him. Our strengths *and* our weaknesses are for His glory (see 2 Cor. 12:8-10).

Why should we ever emphasize the weaknesses of others or discredit them? We should not. Rather we should emphasize the glory of God which is in others. This is His interest and it should be ours.

Give glory to God by your involvement with other people. They need to see how God has blessed them and gifted them personally. It is a blessing to both the giver and the receiver to acknowledge this gift from God. It is an easy thing to see and point out the strengths of others. Such encouragement can lift up the recipients in both self-image and praise to God. It establishes them in the true perspective of God and rejects the lies that make them anything less.

God is great! And as He does His creative and redemptive work in our lives, that greatness is reflected in us. It is really healing to say,

> God's great!
> I'm great!
> You're great!

How Do *You* Identify?

I'm great! It's almost too hard to say, isn't it? Especially after all of those Bible verses we memorized when we were children, like "Pride goes before destruction, a haughty spirit before a fall" (Prov. 16:18), and "Do not think of yourself more highly than you ought, but rather think of yourself with sober judgment, in accordance with the measure of faith God has given you" (Rom. 12:3).

And yet, the words *I'm great* do have a tremendous amount of power within them.

How many of us in the Church today really understand

what we communicate to others through the power of the spoken word? The words of our Lord Jesus carried much power both physically and spiritually. He spoke and taught in some situations where modern-day preachers would have been lost without the wonders of electronic amplification. He spoke to crowds of thousands on several occasions without the use of a microphone. And lives were changed because of His words.

The writer James also reminds us that our words go forth from our hearts and lips with much power. Words themselves may be short and sweet, but they, like the bit in a horse's mouth or a ship's rudder, can change and alter the direction of another person's life (see James 3:3-5). What we say, even in passing, may have a profound effect on the lives of so many people.

Our new next-door neighbors can become our friends or our enemies, just as a result of the tone in our greeting on the way to the mailbox. The check-out clerk at the corner grocery store, struggling to get through a bad day, can have his spirit lifted, or further depressed, by our very attitudes and words. Casual acquaintances begin to label us in their own minds as individuals they either want to know or avoid like the plague, as a result of just a few words from our lips that may make or break their day.

I'm great! You're great! The words themselves are not that meaningful, but their intention and the attitude they project are indeed powerful enough to positively or negatively affect the lives of others.

With that in mind, members of the Body of Christ would do well to gain a sense of responsibility over the words they utter. Knowing that casual remarks could deeply hurt another's self-image, or build up that self-image, we need to take care, and guard our tongues. We all have days when we wake up not exactly in love with the world, feeling the pressures of our jobs, itching for a good argument. Did you ever hear the words, "If you can't say anything nice, don't say anything at all"? That may be sound advice for the days when we are far enough away from the Lord in our walk that we have no intentions of building up the Body of Christ with kind words and positive attitudes.

Instead of talking, maybe we need to be reading. The book of Psalms might help us establish a more pleasant attitude towards life and our Lord, an attitude that might cause the words we speak to others to build them up instead of tear them down.

Members of the Body must also realize that not only does God use our strengths to minister to others, He uses our imperfections as well. Because we have suffered hurts and rejections in certain areas of our lives, we are able to minister to others suffering from those same hurts and rejections. Our imperfections allow us to become effective ministers, because we have been there.

And, finally, as members of the Body of Christ, we need to remember that our own self-image is not necessarily God's image of us. And that gives us hope! On those days when we're not happy with ourselves and the gloom begins to set in, we need to be thankful that the Lord doesn't see us through our own eyes. He sees us through the eyes of His Son Jesus Christ! God cares for us so much that He sent His only Son to save us! And you know, that should make us feel as if we indeed are great. Maybe that's because the God who loves each and every one of us is the *greatest!*

10

The Judas Kiss: Betrayal In the Ministry

Have you ever felt betrayal? Jesus did. In fact, He knew beforehand Judas was going to betray Him. Even so, He washed Judas's feet at the Last Supper. Could we take a lesson from that dramatic story as we deal with betrayal in our own lives? Surely this pastor learned from personal experience the pains of betrayal and the foot-washing joy of forgiveness.

Sometimes I wish that God had made my arms about a foot longer or at least put two-way hinges on my elbows. That would certainly make it a lot easier to reach some of those knives that have been stuck right in the middle of my back. But it wouldn't make it any less painful, would it?

I had spent hours with Andrew, and all I got for it was a sore spot that continued to hurt every time I thought of him. I took time to counsel with him, disciple him in the faith and spent hours teaching him. I met with him every week and poured myself into him. Our church even supported him financially through college and seminary. Now he was back, planting a church in our area for another denomination and inviting the members of our congregation to attend his Bible study.

I noticed over the weeks that a severe attitude change was taking place in those who came under Andrew's influence. They became critical opponents of our church's pastors and of our style of ministry. Andrew was viewed as a strong leader while I was viewed as weak. He was a deep teacher while I was a shallow "storyteller." He was doctrinally pure and sound, but I was regarded as a compromiser, afraid of people and their possible reaction to doctrinal stances.

I could feel that knife in the middle of my back as I walked down the hill the few hundred yards from the church to the parsonage. I had walked that path a thousand times in the past seven years, but this walk was somehow more painful. My thoughts were now fixed on one burning question: "Did Jesus wash Judas's feet at the Last Supper?" I should have known the answer, but I wondered, did Judas excuse himself from the table before the towel and basin were used? Surely, Jesus would dismiss the betrayer before He did His work of compassion and service. No, I determined, the Bible couldn't say that the Lord washed the feet of Judas!

Once into the parsonage, I reached for my Bible and found that John 13 described the scene, vividly and poignantly. Jesus finishes the supper, lays aside His robes, wraps Himself in a towel, kneels and washes His disciples' feet. Here are the symbols of the Kingdom, the tokens of ministry, the attitudes of service. And then, a few verses later we find the words, "One of you is going to betray me" (John 13:21). Only then was Judas dispatched on his infamous journey.

Although my mind recoiled at the thought, the answer was yes, Jesus had washed "those feet" on that last night, and He knew what was going to happen. I might be spared that particular problem of knowing beforehand, but the implications were only too clear to me, who had been betrayed in ministry. I was going to have to wash some feet. "I have set you an example . . . . Now that you know these things, you will be blessed if you do them" (John 13:15,17).

The ministry often calls us to the banqueting room of betrayal. The psalmist has said it: "You prepare a table before me in the presence of my enemies" (Ps. 23:5). A strange environment for a feast. Yet it happens that, "Even my close friend, whom I trusted, he who shared my bread, has lifted up his heel against me" (Ps. 41:9).

Any pastor who has long loved and labored is especially broken in betrayal. Any idealism of faith, hope and trust is torn from top to bottom. The mind does suffer an insurrection, and here indeed is a crisis of faith. "Where have I failed? What was my sin? What more could I have done? Are they right?"

This is not just a difference of opinion. You have walked in faithfulness and ministered in integrity. But now those you love turn in angry accusation with words that lacerate and sting.

The nature of betrayal in the ministry is difficult to analyze because it assumes various forms. The common denominator seems to be personal emotional investment, often over a long period of time, with ministry which is often shared, much like the scriptural pattern of Jesus and

Judas. A pattern that is complete with its shared intimacy of the inner circle, decision to defect and ultimate betrayal. This final act is consummated with the Judas kiss—intimacy exploited in public denunciation.

In ministry, the bonds of unity and love are the cords that hold us in relationship with God's people. Pastors don't and shouldn't emotionally invest themselves in every single person, but ministry is more than the task. Otherwise, pastoring would be more like gardening than shepherding; it's a lot easier to lose a pumpkin than a lamb.

In Jesus' ministry the disciples learned, lived and loved together. In the local church we drink deeply of the water of life. The reciprocity of ministry gives it its flavor and is based on trust. The depth of the agony of betrayal can only be fully known by those who have also known the profound joy of Christian love.

Ann and Al were one of the most attractive couples in the church. We were attracted to them that first Sunday we candidated at the church, and it didn't take long for us to become good friends. We had Bible studies together in our homes; we went out to dinner together; we had our first children together. We encouraged them as they started their own business, and we stood beside them when it failed. Ann even told me that she thought that I truly had the gift of wisdom. But now she was telling me that she didn't get anything out of church. She complained that my sermons had too many stories, and that she really had some doubts about my theological convictions.

Our love for Ann and Al was deep, which made the pain of their betrayal all the more intense. Make no mistake; Judas was one of the 12 in every perceivable way, which makes his decision that much more horrible. It seems a matter of course that the Pharisees would plot and scheme, but when it is done by someone closer than a brother it is an utter violation.

Being done in by your auto mechanic seems much lower on the scale than a friend's stab in the back. And it doesn't ever seem to stop there. Others get drawn into the web of conspiracy, sometimes beginning with those meetings where people have gathered to "pray for the pastor."

If the minister is fortunate, the former devotee will come to him privately and agree to disagree. There may be sharp disavowal, but it is contained. The public turning of the worm is another matter.

John had come to faith through the efforts of my ministry. I had the opportunity to walk with him through a messy divorce and had spent a lot of time listening to him and encouraging him in his growth as a Christian. But now, I found that he was attracted to some very rigid and legalistic teachings, perhaps as a result of a confused and troubled past. The upshot of it all was his public denunciation of me before our church diaconate: "This man allows young people to listen to rock and roll; he sees nothing wrong with them having a beer; and now some people in this church even subscribe to cable television."

Such a public attack on the pastor is much like that favorite motif in art history, the public betrayal of Jesus by Judas known as "The Judas Kiss." It is the awful irony of a tender gesture bespeaking untold depths of hurt, malice, treachery, and it is only the beginning. So often the poison spreads, infecting friends, marriages, families and sometimes other churches. The pastor endures sleepless nights; days of depression; tears for breakfast, lunch and dinner; and often broken health.

For instance, one recent sleepless night included

replays of the week's counseling sessions: the marriage betrayed by an affair, the church member in court for domestic violence, the hospital visits to the locked ward and a recent accusation that the church has become luke-warm. Is it no wonder that guilt and doubt begin to take up residence in a pastor's life along with the constant question, "Why?"

Let's turn to Jesus as we mull that question over in our hearts and minds. Ponder His betrayal and where it led, and when we have asked ourselves every possible combination of the "Why me?" question, we need to look upon the Crucified One and ask, "Why not me?"

Next, we will turn to the Scriptures. Listen, and God will speak to us as never before. "A broken and contrite heart, O God, you will not despise" (Ps. 51:17). God is much closer. Isaiah, Joseph and Job will befriend us. The flame is designed to burn dross *and* refine gold, and though people have broken us, people will mend us, too.

The day after one of the greatest blows in my early Christian life, I was sitting with Byron, a retired mission-ary friend. I was feeling crushed and betrayed. I had invested my life in a relationship with a young lady named Patty. We grew close to one another, and spent time in prayer about our life together and had come to the conclu-sion that it was a commitment that would last a lifetime. We became engaged; then after almost a year, the engage-ment had fallen apart.

Byron felt impressed to tell me a story from his experi-ence in the mission field. In Africa, he had been given charge over the hammer mill, where the grain was pounded to a very fine flour. If rain damaged a crop, the process was abbreviated, some of the hammering reduced and a coarser grain of flour produced. Inevitably the nationals touch-tasting the flour would protest, "If our people eat that flour it will make them sick." Now, the flour was perfect to the eye and certainly suitable for use, but the difference was in the tasting. Byron looked me right in the eye and said, "Spencer, you can go through life protected from the hammering process. You will be a minister of the gospel, but in breaking the Bread of Life to the people of God, the difference will be in the tasting."

God can and will bring something out of this chastening of betrayal. We may learn more of ourselves in some of the pain of experience, for there may be some truth related to the charges made. It has been said that "our enemies are the most direct path to the truth," and of course it is precisely here that the analogy between pairs—Jesus/Judas and the pastor/the "plotter"—breaks down. Jesus was truly sinless, and no charges were made that could stick. We are sinners, and while we may be ready to hold fast to the philosophy of letting those who are without sin cast the first stone as a means for preventing us from bodily harm, we must still be ready to catch a few of those stones!

But how do we handle such a barrage? Sticks and stones do break bones, and names do hurt. Names like "compromiser" and words like "weak," "lukewarm," "too busy" and "unavailable" can sometimes hurt for a very long time.

Consider the source of attack. Is it a doctrinal dispute? It usually is: well then, is it a doctrinal issue central to the faith? It usually isn't, but they think it is.

Is the Church going to topple to the left or right on this pivotal issue? Sometimes it literally seems as if it will. It is this division between spiritual and unspiritual, between second-class and first-class Christianity, which so saps energy, narrows the bigger picture and plays into the ene-my's divisional tactics.

When an individual in the local church begins a cam-paign to establish unanimity on one of the issues not cen-tral to faith in Christ, division of some sort is inevitable. How many churches have been split over those major doc-trinal issues so central to the faith as baptism, means of grace, use of gifts or what color to paint the church vestry? Individuals need to decide what constitutes the kernel of faith and what are simply peripheral issues of truth. It is when that individual concern, that pet issue becomes what everyone in the church must have in order to be a true believer, that most of the people and usually the pastor, end up unhappy.

People in the church should be able to debate doctrine, and when some differences of opinion arise over a heart-felt issue, then often it is best for someone to leave the church. Usually it is the person or persons who are exer-cised over the issue; sometimes it is the pastor. When someone becomes valiant-for-truth however, then nothing less than a white tornado seems to have hit the church. How much better when the departure is done decently and in order, much like slipping out of a room. It is when the doors start slamming and the voices are rising that it gets ugly.

Another aspect of betrayal revolves around the cult of personality. The pastor who realizes he cannot be all things to all people feels the sting of the Judas kiss when unrealistic demands are made of him. Some of those demands and expectations seem endless.

The pastor must be a great expository preacher, a gifted evangelist, a psychotherapist, a guru, a handsome—and zippy—youth leader, a sensitive senior citizens' man, a glib and glossy speaker, a soft-spoken zealot who really *wants* to live in a shack and work for nothing. It is obviously impossible to meet all these expectations, partly because so many identities can't fit into one shack! Paul himself, after enumerating his sufferings for the gospel, adds to the list, "I face daily the pressure of my concern for all the churches" (2 Cor. 11:28). No doubt he felt the burden of unfulfilled expectations. People can turn in anger on a pastor when their particular agenda has not been met.

Problems can also arise when political power-brokers within the church become unhappy. This is especially true in smaller churches that begin to experience growth. Those who have held the reins and pulled the strings now face a narrowing power base, and this threatening turn of events can turn the pastor into a scapegoat. This last image is a good one to keep in mind, for the pastor is the person who truly does bear the blame for many in his congregation.

I remember the church treasurer who has held tightly to the purse strings and exploded at the suggestion that the church needs a part-time secretary. The pastor receives the tongue lashing—"You can't get blood out of a stone!"—while the treasurer storms out of the church in tears. And nothing tests the power of those who wish to hold it like the suggestion from a new member that the church undergo remodeling or renovations. That is one area that is sure to lead to hurt feelings and explosive situations because it means change, and for those who are in power, that can be threatening. In the midst of some sort of confusing emotional crisis the pastor oftens stumbles about, feeling lost and driven from any known haven of rest and security.

Another aspect of betrayal in ministry springs from emotional blame-shifting, often done by people with some deep-seated problems. The pastor is accused of hypocrisy by the board member who at home is beating his wife and children. The pastor is perceived as a weak leader by the unhappy woman married to a difficult man. A lonely, emotionally-starved individual accuses the pastor of not meeting any needs. The parent with rebellious children blames the minister for not spending enough time with the youth ministry.

The list seems endless, but the pastor who experiences the Judas kiss must look behind the criticism and evaluate the source. This is hard to do when the pastor is relatively new to a congregation, but in time, one learns to be a mirror to the people, reflecting their hurts, frustrations and bitter disappointments. The flaming hurt of criticism is part of the refining fire and will give the pastor an even greater ability to reflect to his people the truth of shared suffering, that strange alchemy that exchanges beauty for ashes, crowns for thorns.

One of the best pastoral analogies I have ever heard likened congregational criticism to colic. Sometimes the pastor will simply have to let someone burp on him, much like a mother who burps the baby in order to prevent or alleviate discomfort. Like Paul, pastors are midwives to their congregations, working hard to help shape these lives into the image of Christ. It is usually a painful struggle, as those who have experienced or watched birth know very well.

I have attended the birth of each one of my children, and I vividly recall the first birth, a very long and difficult one. Instead of the team effort we had so long rehearsed in Lamaze class, my wife regarded me as an extremely irritating distraction in the room, fit only for the spooning of ice chips into the royal mouth. I was told not to watch TV, not to rustle the newspapers, not to talk to her, not to help time the contractions and finally to "just go away." What was to have been a shared experience of glorious cooperation turned into 25 hours of hard work on her part and bored fatigue on mine. To this day she cannot explain the change, only that she needed to concentrate, and I was like a pea in a mattress.

Did I feel betrayed? Perhaps, but I was the logical one on which to vent some very full feelings. And the pastor is, too. After all, in the crassest sense, it is what you get paid for, while holding in tension the opposite thought that no amount of money in the world could repay all that you do.

Betrayal in the ministry is a monster with many heads. It can be discussed, analyzed, dissected and codified, but like every other life experience—birth, marriage, grief, learning to ride a bicycle—it cannot be truly known until it happens. And it does happen. There can be no protection from it, if the pastor truly has a heart for his calling.

Unsubstantiated betrayal—especially when it takes the guise of a parishioner who smiles and smiles, and yet is a villain—is one of the surest ways to get a pastor to put on some protective, unbiblical armor. Resist that temptation. Let Jesus remove any layers of time-toughened skin from a hardened heart. One of the best ways is to continue to serve those who have determined your betrayal. Reach for the towel and the basin, and wash their feet. There can be reconciliation with the betrayer.

A pastor friend recently confided a special joy. A family had left his church years ago amidst angry accusations of his supposed theological compromises and departure from orthodoxy. Now, years later, the pastor found himself in conversation with his betrayers and almost as an afterthought one of them said, "Pastor, it isn't until recently that I have come to realize the pain we caused you and your wife. Please forgive me."

Don't look for apologies to come; they usually won't. But it is a very sweet thing when they do, sweeter because they are unlooked for. It is up to the pastor to practice what he preaches: "If it is possible, as far as it depends on you, live at peace with everyone" (Rom. 12:18).

Reconciliation is possible, but even if you get left in the Garden of Gethsemane, you will be better for it. The difference will be in the tasting. "Taste and see that the Lord is good" (Ps. 34:8).

How Do *You* Identify?

The pain of betrayal has been and always will be part of the territory when it comes to ministry. Since church congregations are comprised of people functioning on various levels of spiritual maturity (and spiritual immaturity) it is unrealistic to believe that everyone will always see eye to eye on all spiritual matters. If that is the case, it is important for those sitting in the pew as well as those standing behind the pulpit, to gain a better understanding on how to deal with one another as we all suffer the pain of intentional and unintentional betrayal.

In the book of Ephesians, Paul tells us, "It was he who gave some to be apostles, some to be prophets, some to be evangelists, and some to be pastors and teachers"

(Eph. 4:11). Paul was referring to the gifting and calling of certain members of the Body into leadership roles. But we need to note that the subject of the verse, "some", the ones who are called, are human beings. Pastors are people, too. And as people, they have feelings and emotions which often affect, shape and sometimes limit how they approach individuals and problems.

Those believers who are called by God to be lay members of the Body of Christ might do well to remember that those called into leadership positions in the Church are not immune from heartache, sorrow and disappointment simply because they are busy doing the Lord's work. The Lord's work calls them into contact with other human beings who share similar imperfections and shortcomings. A bit of understanding for a pastor who is suffering the pain of betrayal or from a broken relationship goes a long way to ease the hurt.

A sound point to remember is that pastors who seek transparency often leave themselves open for painful personal relationships. The apostle Paul was able to have a tremendous effect on people because of his "transparent" style and approach to ministry, which he describes as, "I have become all things to all men so that by all possible means I might save some" (1 Cor. 9:22). Life is shared and ministry is carried on at a deeper, more personal level. Members of the Body receive the care of their shepherd on a more intimate level.

But members also discover that a pastor's gifts, time and patience, like theirs, is not endless. Pastors who sometimes face situations and problems for which they have no ready answers may suddenly seem to be out of touch with those to whom they were once close. Inability to come up with instant cures may be translated by the flock as a lack of compassion and willingness to understand. Pastors don't love any less because they may have no answers, but it may be difficult when you are hurting to remember that. As a result, a once transparent pastor may be open to criticism which may not be warranted, but painful just the same.

As believers we need to also understand that betrayal and pain sometimes occur when we seek to solve problems without going through biblical channels. No church is free from problems and because of that fact, the New Testament gives us guidelines for handling such matters and disputes. Paul says, "Brothers, if someone is caught in a sin, you who are spiritual should restore him gently" (Gal. 6:1). Our tendency, however, is to omit the word *gently* as we sometimes seek to solve and remove problems surgically and at the same time cut off members from the body. For any single member, pastor or lay person, to deal with problems or problem people in such a manner may cause more pain and a sense of betrayal to the Body as a whole and may require a longer period of healing than if the problem were handled according to biblical procedure.

Finally, we need to note that actual betrayal within the Church may come as a result of the nature of some congregations. To be realistic, we must admit that not every person who is a member of the Church is a member of the Body of Christ. Honesty permits us to acknowledge the fact that not every church member or individual holding a church leadership role has a personal relationship with Jesus Christ.

Believers and unbelievers are not always going to see eye to eye, especially when it comes to spiritual matters. The Psalmist tells us, "How good and pleasant it is when brothers live together in unity!" (Ps. 133:1). And yet, as long as human beings who are unwilling to accept one another in all their strengths and weaknesses make up the Church, such unity may be a long time in coming. The result is inevitable; there will be plenty of room and potential for "The Judas Kiss."

11

The Great Weasel Hunt

His outlook on life was different than that of the Cree Indians to whom he would soon minister. How would the culture and customs of the Crees influence this pastor's ability to present the gospel? We will soon find out when he makes his first visit into the bush country of northern Quebec. He goes to pastor and ends up in "the great weasel hunt!"

––––––––––

Actually, the plane ride wasn't bad. I had plenty of room to stretch out in the back of the DeHavillon Beaver. The frigid subarctic air swirling into the plane through the cargo door that wouldn't close kept my nausea at bay.

Looking out the plane window, whenever I mustered the nerve, I saw an endless panorama of lakes and trees cut only by the occasional snowshoe or snowmobile trail. A dizzying circle around a barely visible log lodge gave an opportunity to see a thin line of smoke rising into the blue.

The family I had come to visit was at home.

This was to be for me the first of many pastoral visits among the Cree trappers in the bush country of northern Quebec. My view of ministry, the church, prayer and fellowship began to change on that very first trip. All that I had experienced of Christian faith and practice would be challenged through my ministry to the Crees.

Having heroically survived my first bush plane ride, I looked forward to an enthusiastic greeting, as I stepped out onto the frozen lake. Instead, reserved smiles, few words and a single handshake from all present greeted me. Once inside the neat lodge and comfortably seated on the spruce-bough floor, I tried to appear relaxed.

"Tea?"

"Yes, thanks! That plane was cold!"

A logical explanation came quickly from an astonished young face, "It's winter."

Tea came and I was glad for the diversion. Realizing that the tea had been drawn from a pot in which two little boys had been floating wooden boats, I was prepared to chew, if necessary.

Suddenly, two older men burst into the lodge yelling directions in Cree and moving everyone to a huge woodpile outside. I was handed a substantial piece of wood. My Cree was good enough to know that I was to hit "it" as soon as I saw "it," but not good enough to know what "it" would be. As the woodpile was demolished stick by stick, anticipation grew. Between bits of Cree and English, I managed to learn that there was a fine little weasel hiding in the woodpile. The camp boss wanted to catch it for his granddaughter so that she could sell its hide to the fur trader when he came to camp.

Suddenly, my thoughts of how foolish we all looked

jumping around a woodpile in our shirtsleeves at minus 30 degrees were sobered by the gravity of my responsibility. Whether or not this little girl would have a weasel skin to sell rested in my rapidly freezing hands. As the woodpile got smaller, everyone else apparently began to reassess the wisdom of giving me the central task. I was relieved of my club and instructed to remove logs slowly from the remaining pile.

With only a dozen logs remaining, the two older men drew closer, steeling for the strike. I attempted to remove logs as slowly as possible so as not to scare the weasel, but also to avoid being clubbed should it suddenly appear. It did. Like a white blur, it jumped out of the woodpile and into the jacket of one of the two men, who began dancing around, yelling and slapping his chest and his back. The other man looked for a clear swing with his club that would do his friend Billy as little harm as possible and yet dispatch the weasel.

In the mayhem, the weasel slipped out of Billy's jacket and escaped into a nearby snow bank. The weasel was unharmed. I was unharmed. Isaiah was disappointed. And the rest of the camp was too weak from laughter to move. Through my own laughter, I realized that this little hunt had ruined my plans for this first visit.

The short time that the plane could sit grounded in the frigid cold was gone. I left the lodge in disappointment, hardly noticing the beauty around me. I was inclined to think that these people did not really want a visit centered around the gospel. But to my surprise, just before I climbed in through the door, the young girl who had lost her weasel brought me a package of moose meat and enough fur and cash to more than pay for my entire plane trip. "Thank you for the visit and for your help. My grandfather says thanks, too. Please visit us again." On the way to the next camp, I barely noticed the cold as I tried to figure out what had just taken place.

That weasel hunt had cut right across my plans and expectations. Similar scenarios occurred throughout my five years of ministry in northern Quebec. I was experiencing a cross-cultural ministry.

I found, however, the more I compared notes with those in ministry to their own culture, the more similarities I found to my northern ministry. Bible studies that terminated for no apparent reason, worship that upset long-standing parishioners, tension between members on the parish board, whole families that suddenly began to participate when nothing appeared to have changed in the church, programs that thrived and grew with little effort while others never got off the ground, all represented an elusive element of parish life that I had assumed was based on different cultural outlooks. It occurred to me that the cause for some of the unwanted frustration and the unexpected joy in ministry was not based nearly as much upon pastoral skills, resources, facilities and adequate support, as upon perception of the gospel in relation to everyday life. Slowly, I began to realize how much my ministry, all ministry, has to do with personal perceptions of Christianity and life in general.

Where I felt that first visit to be the middle of nowhere, the family saw their camp to be a comfortable home in the midst of familiar rocks, trees, streams and beaver houses. Their greeting seemed cool to me, but to them, they had been exuberant. My outlook on life was different from theirs. It followed that the things I found most important in the gospel would be different from what they found to be important in life and living.

Understanding differing perceptions of the gospel and applying that understanding to ministry suddenly became very important to me. I had to look far beyond the bounds of worship or fellowship to understand the new outlook presented to me in the Cree village. I had always thought that one's life was influenced by one's Christian faith. To some extent, I saw this to be true as Christian maturity grew in my parishioners.

I had to admit, however, that often, exactly the opposite was true for me as a pastor. My life, home environment, my citizenship, my education and a myriad of other influences had determined a great deal of my Christian faith and practice. Ministry in a new culture was not the difficulty. Rather, I was hampered by my own inability to separate Christianity from my life, myself.

Certainly, in ministry, differences of opinion arise and separate on doctrinal, liturgical, canonical and pastoral issues. However, we must realize that there are those who find it difficult to relate to Christianity at all. There are those who misunderstand the message and the motive of the gospel and never take that step of receiving Christ by faith, and not as a matter of conscience, but because of an opposing perception of the gospel in their own life.

Two forces, each related to the other, created tension in my ministry and life in northern Quebec until I identified them. These forces are acting in every life, in every church. I have chosen to call them culture and custom. These two forces are seen in the extreme in a cross-cultural setting and are very much bound up in all ministry, all interpersonal relationships and all business transactions within any culture, new or familiar.

By culture, I am referring to those things which occur daily, constantly in a society influenced by the past and the environment and social structure of the present. Culture is continually changing in order to adapt to the future needs of a society while remaining grounded in the past for a degree of stability. Cultural influences mean security and a source of stability for groups operating within that society.

If ignored, circles of cultural influence can cause terrible fragmentation in any social group. For example, permanent homes in Cree villages in the north have done a lot to destroy the stability of the very village. From the southern point of view this seems to be ridiculous. However, when the search for housing and the work to maintain that house become a major part of life, permanent housing can be seen to have some bad effects on a people who thrive on the mobility of the family unit into and out of the bush country.

Culture defines family, societal structures, recreation, educational patterns and standards, religious practices and almost every other area of life. Culture seems to be the easiest thing for an outsider to ignore, particularly when armed with a zealous desire to preach the gospel according to one's own chosen style and pattern. It is because of this tendency that culture is an important force to identify in order to enhance the effect of any ministry.

Custom, on the other hand, is a much more local, specialized adaptation of culture. It is built and regulated by small groups and spheres of influence within the larger culture. "Church," for example, builds custom into the cultural patterns of members. Families develop customary celebrations within cultural holiday times. Workers build custom for themselves or their work unit within a cultural framework to aid in doing their job. Custom and culture shape, to a degree, every community and every social grouping within each community. It follows that Christian faith and practice must also be shaped by these forces.

In northern Quebec, the Cree people are of one culture somewhat isolated from other cultures that might influence life. When I went North to minister, the cultural clash was obvious in everything from my sense of humor to my ability to get lost instantly in the bush. My customary outlook on everything from food preparation to liturgical practice was at odds with that of the people around me. Differences could be identified and dealt with.

In many parishes, cultural and customary differences may be far less obvious but just as real. The pastor needs to be aware of these forces in all areas of parish life. This is especially true of the pastor moving to a new ministry. Style of prayer, emphasis in teaching, study group structure, tools used, place of meeting, types of greetings and hundreds of other things outside the direct scope of Christian teaching can make or break a pastoral call, a fellowship evening or an entire ministry.

Anyone ministering in Christ's name ministers through a personal context of both custom and culture. This is only natural. If it is unrecognized, it can be harmful to the ministry. Most resistance to ministry begins as some form of the familiar is changed or threatened by change. The same pastoral prayer relocated in the service may not be acknowledged. Familiar teaching through new examples may be rejected at first. The minister brings personal custom and culture to ministry as much as personal theology, liturgical practice or biblical understanding.

As an Anglican pastor, I found myself using a prayer book for Cree worship which was translated from a book written in 1662. Weekly intercessions for world leaders were made using a prayer from this book directing the congregation to pray for a monarch long since dead. However, the first Sunday that I omitted the printed name and added the name of the present English monarch, many people in the congregation asked me not to change the prayers. After a bit of teaching and discussion, our intercessions became more relevant. It appeared that in this case, content was not the question but that the familiar was at issue.

A brief look at the ministry of Jesus reveals that He experienced difficulty at the hands of religious leaders as He demonstrated God's love apart from the cultural and customary norms of the day. He challenged people to understand again the intent of God's Law as He cut through the cultural fences built to protect the community of Israel. He ministered beyond the customary bounds of propriety by going to those people who had been shut out by custom. He challenged those who had customarily abused the holy principle of sacrifice, offering it for their own gain only and ignoring the link with God that it offered. He confronted those who justified their own actions by customarily condemning the actions of others.

Jesus did not bring a new message; rather, He attempted to help people look through centuries of custom and ritual back to a relationship with their God in personal terms. His sacrifice was necessary, as the death of God's Son is powerful enough to allow us to cut through custom and culture to see God. The Christian faith and its practice becomes clouded by culture and custom at this point. I was startled one day as a young man asked me if I would consider teaching sometime on the subject of the Christian faith. What had I been doing all along? He saw something that I had not! My culture shining through my idea of Christianity was making the gospel irrelevant to him.

If we stop and think about our use of Scripture, we

realize that we are constantly making customary and cultural adaptations. To suggest slavery as a norm for North American society would be abhorrent. We understand this cultural aspect of the gospel and examine the truth within. It is just as important to examine the day-to-day trappings that we have added to our Christian faith because of our culture and custom.

A pastor must know whether the customary and cultural workings of Christian practice in a parish are being undercut or used as a vehicle for the gospel. This is not an easy task in a parish made up of many different cultural backgrounds and customary preferences. My own ability to minister to the Cree Indians grew more effective as I identified my own cultural prejudices in Christian faith and practice.

This brings up an interesting point. Who should be adapting to whose culture or custom? Should the congregation as a whole or in part meet the expectations of the pastor, or should the pastor set aside, as much as possible, his or her cultural expression of the gospel to minister more effectively? I could not really offer the Crees of Quebec a gospel that would work in their daily lives until I first understood their daily lives. It seems to me that the pastor must adapt to the needs of the people in whole or in part as their lives require. The apostle Paul's injunction that we are to become "all things to all men" (1 Cor. 9:22, *RSV*) takes on a new meaning as we attempt to see both cultural and customary patterns within a Christian fellowship. For the gospel to affect a life, it must fit into that life. Attempting to weed out, if only temporarily, those things more cultural and customary than Christian from my Christian perspective, I discovered the gospel in a way that I had never known or experienced before.

The concept of the tithe seemed ridiculous in a culture where "things" were not at a premium. I had hoped to preach the Old Testament concept of time and talent because I had always heard it and believed in it. My parishioners were willing to give anything when needed, much as the New Testament suggests. I attempted to teach decorum within the confines of the church building. My parishioners attempted to teach me the reverence of God in creation. I diligently taught the meaning of the Eucharist, while my older parishioners attempted to show me how they learned of Christ's sacrifice in terms of the animals who died to keep them from starving.

The New England village that seems hard to penetrate, the inner-city block where doors won't open, the suburban neighborhood with its complex relationship to the city and the conservative farming community where people stand on self-sufficiency all have customary adaptations for dealing with life. Identifying and accepting these adaptations is crucial for successful ministry.

Just as the pastor must recognize the forces of culture and custom in the ministry, parishioners must also acknowledge these forces in order to successfully apply the gospel to their own lives. Because so many spheres of influence bring custom and culture to life, ministry tends to grow from level to level in Christian living. This is not as much a matter of growing in faith as a matter of a growing confidence to apply faith to culture and customary norms. The further away from "church" a sphere of influence may be found, the less Christian faith and practice will be a part of relating to that sphere.

In northern Quebec, the spirituality of the hunting culture has greatly influenced Christian spirituality. For this reason, all of life is incorporated in Christian living. There are certainly the failures to overcome temptations and all of the difficulties encountered anywhere in Christian living. However, no part of life is seen as unrelated to the gospel. In villages where hunting as a culture is dying, faith also plays a diminishing role in life.

Often, in our modern society, only that compartment of life designated as "religious" has customs which lend themselves to things of the faith. Many spheres of influence may have a place for some Christian practice, but only a maturity of faith enables a person to do a specifically Christian thing in a specifically non-Christian area of life. For example, people who regularly give thanks for meals at home may find themselves reluctant to do so at McDonalds. The sports figure who gives thanks to God in public is noticed by all, not so much for the message, but for the cultural or customary place in which that message is presented. For this reason, many Christians have found that custom has defined the place for Christians to practice their faith.

In a pluralistic society, many priorities with their own customary and cultural patterns make it difficult for the pastor or the parishioner to concentrate on Christian living in a relevant way. The culture whose main priority is to stay close to God will appear far different from that whose priority is to have a multitude of possessions. I was a bit embarrassed when my Christian conviction was seriously questioned in the North simply because I went fishing on a Sunday. In a society where killing to survive is a way of life, Sundays were seen as a break both for the hunter and the hunted. What a dilemma! I was living in a fisherman's paradise, with only Sunday afternoons free for fishing, in a society in which fishing on Sunday was unacceptable.

I was forced very early in my northern ministry to

determine how much of my faith was gospel and how much was cultural interpretation. Everyone approaches the gospel where it most meets life, but everyone must clearly understand what it is of their faith that is gospel and what is application. Difficulty in ministry arises when this separation is not understood by both the pastor and the parishioner. I had always assumed that reverence for animals as fellow occupants of this world was somewhat animistic until I met people who considered me to be pagan because of my limited outlook of the world around me.

Interwoven into each life is custom and culture. For Christian faith to become a working part of life, it must become a part of the pattern of custom and culture. A pastor often needs to set aside personal customary Christian expression to enable parishioners to practice their faith in all areas of life.

Each pastor must approach ministry aware of his or her background. Influences of the past and aspirations for the future all result in change in our perceptions of the gospel. I was at a loss at more than one weasel hunt, attempting to understand why the gospel I knew and loved was so hard to share. Once I realized that the gospel was different than the things in my life that helped me learn and grow as a Christian, my ministry began to take shape.

Unfortunately, at times, it is easier to do the thing that is most customary or most cultural even if it cuts across the gospel. This is the opposite side of the tension. The pastor must know when to draw the line for the sake of the gospel. One cannot simply accept all that is customary within a parish without first subjecting teaching, worship and fellowship patterns to the gospel itself.

As I now approach ministry, I attempt to understand these two forces from both my perspective and that of the parish, particularly in three specific areas. Perhaps the most visible of these three is the area of worship. Nothing in parish life among the Cree Indians is more important than worship patterns. Changes do come, but with teaching and understanding. The same could be said of most congregations, as well.

Parish structure is a second area very much determined by culture and custom. Families often hold traditional offices or positions. Study groups may have traditional nights to meet. All would seem easy enough to change and yet, all seem, at times, to be unchangeable. No logical explanation can be given at times for parish or church structure. It just is, and sometimes just plain should be.

The third area that I attempt to view from the perspective of culture and custom is parish fellowship. Most parishioners might not be willing to acknowledge that there are specific patterns in this area, but many church members and churches as a whole have very rigid fellowship patterns. These patterns may include family lines, lines of seniority within the parish, age groups and vocation groups, to name a few. The consistent changing of these patterns, whatever they might be, could disrupt parish life.

This brief examination of the forces of culture and custom in the life of a parish is only an attempt to alert the pastor and parishioner to the forces at work within the life of a church which may often go on unidentified but not undetected.

Each pastor is at work in a "cross-cultural" setting to one degree or another. Each pastor has times when a "weasel hunt" cuts across plans and brings disappointment or offers surprises through unforeseen results. Alert and accurate readings of cultural and customary influences on parish life can, however, make Christian teaching and fellowship more relevant in day-to-day living.

It is not enough to walk away from a "weasel hunt" saying, "Never again!" or "Why me?" The pastor should try to understand why the weasel hunt took place to begin with. It may be that weasel hunting is more important to our parishioners than we could ever imagine.

How Do *You* Identify?

How many fellow believers do you know personally who have recently been involved in a weasel hunt? I don't mean the kind that takes place out by the woodpile with a real, honest-to-goodness, live *Mustelidae frenata* (that's fancy for weasel), but the kind that takes place in life where two cultures cross over and you find yourself at a loss to understand other people, their traditions and how they express their faith in Jesus Christ. The kind of weasel hunt where you attempt to worship or fellowship with a fellow citizen of the family of God who is from a place you can't pronounce. You are members of the same Body of Christ, but barely able to speak the same language.

This is a possibility today for so many churches. Our mobile society allows for most any congregation to be made up of people from a variety of cultural and ethnic backgrounds. Inner-city churches in our nation today are seeing a rising number of new believers who are refugees from Southeast Asia and Latin America. So many of our churches become perfect locations for congregational members to experience a weasel hunt, as fellow members of the Body strive to worship, fellowship and live out their own interpretations of the gospel.

It is true that every pastor is, to some extent, involved in a "cross cultural" ministry. We may not realize it, but we all worship in a "cross cultural" church, be it in the inner-city, the suburbs or the country. We are all living in a society and culture which changes so rapidly, there are times when we may feel as if we have been dropped by a DeHavillon Beaver into another world, but in actuality, we have never left our own neighborhoods.

The world around us changes so fast while the church in which we worship and serve often just plods along at a much slower pace. We become steeped in tradition, and our worship, programs and means for reaching out with the gospel seem to be set in concrete. And when the time finally comes for us to reach out and minister to the real world which surrounds us, or when a member of that world comes into our church for the very first time, it becomes almost a "cross cultural" experience.

Isn't it wonderful then, that we have a "cross cultural" God? The world may change, but God doesn't. People may have different needs and speak different languages, but we have a Christ who died to save us all. As individual members of that Body, each one of us must seek to grow in our relationship with Christ, and through Him, in our relationships with one another. I believe that the weasel hunts of life may be exciting, for at that moment when cultures begin to cross, we experience the opportunity to relate to another brother or sister in Christ, with whom we are at one.

12

A Bicycle and the Family Dog

Six caskets, all in a row. Four small ones, two adult size. Together, the twins shared one of them. Fires that hot don't leave much to bury. Tragedies of this magnitude are supposed to happen somewhere else. But they happened here, and this pastor had the awesome duty to comfort the bereaved and, in the process, try to shape some meaning into it all.

Three of the six children who had died with their mother in that early morning blaze had been members of our youth choir. Perhaps that is one reason I was invited to participate in their funeral, even though the family was Catholic.

George, one of our trustees, had called at 6:30 A.M. on

Wednesday, March 4, 1981. He wanted to let me know there had been a fire. No one had escaped.

"Are they sure?" I asked.

He assured me they were sure. They were searching for the bodies now.

I was there within the hour, viewing a scene that is permanently etched in my mind. Volunteer firemen and others were poking through the rubble, some struggling with the help of a forklift to get to the victims at the basement level.

The mortician, a personal friend, glanced at me as he went about his grim work. He said something like, "I guess you've been through this kind of thing before."

I nodded, but I think something deep within me was disengaged.

One family dog, the sole survivor, loyally guarded a body bag. Still lying amidst the smoldering ruins, in full view, the charred remains of two more victims awaited theirs.

The parish priest slowly made his somber visitations. There were a few other observers, but not many. No big city barricades here. Just small-town country people, doing what demanded doing.

And, because that parish priest and I were the only ministers in the two northern Wisconsin towns directly involved with this tragedy, we not only had freedom of access to the scene, but we also inherited the responsibility of somehow trying to make some sense of all this.

Definitely not a textbook situation!

Almost immediately, I began wrestling with some of the questions. I went home and got out my Bible, looking for answers. Ecclesiastes. Here were some words that made sense! "'Meaningless! Meaningless!' says the

Teacher. 'Utterly meaningless! Everything is meaningless'" (Eccles. 1:2). I read on with interest.

Beyond the horror and the awfulness of the event itself, certain issues began to come into focus over the next several days. Of these, the most significant was a foundational question about reality. On the one hand, when I turned away from that fire scene, I left behind a certain searing, grotesque reality, returning home to one that was far, far more comfortable. But there seemed such a great gulf fixed between the two.

I asked myself, "Which one of these is true?"

Was one of them somehow more real than the other?

A philosopher might approach this question like this:

"Your dreams seem quite real, don't they?"

"Yes, I sometimes wake up in a cold sweat!"

He might continue, "How do you know that, in fact, what we call waking isn't really the dream, and the dream the real thing?"

A solution came to mind from past reading that helped me begin to develop an answer. The waking state is more real, because it is able to contain the other. We can fit the dream inside the waking, but not the reverse. Thus, the waking must be somehow bigger, the more "real" reality, reality with a big R.

Sometimes a certain larger reality breaks through the fog of our normal lives, showing us clearly, but perhaps only for an instant, that what we believe to be reality is, in reality, like a dream compared to waking. These rare opportunities to understand deserve our full attention.

Of course, we can turn away and shortly become immersed in the dream again. But that was not my plan, for myself or the others. We would consider the meaning of this event, before it slipped away. The magnitude of the tragedy demanded it, and the opportunities were not long in coming.

First, there was the student body: six out of around 300 suddenly snuffed out! The principal called, asking if I would address a special memorial service on Friday. There were some, he said, who needed a better understanding of death. Not long after the fire, the students were already arguing over who would get the desk space of the ones who had died. Most children handle death differently than adults, and it's probably unrealistic to expect differently, but when the time for the memorial service arrived, I wanted to be able to help everyone focus on what lessons there might be in this event for those of us who remained.

How could I help them glimpse the bigger reality, the things of eternal significance, while at the same time face head-on the awful reality of what had just occurred?

I knew flowery poetry and philosophical sayings were not the answer to the confusion some of them might be experiencing. While these might help to cover over or wish away the nature of this tragedy, long term they would prove ineffective in dealing with it.

They were all there, first to twelfth grade, teachers, administrators, even one TV crew; this was a major event for our rural area. As I began, I wanted to set two truths side by side:

> One: death is ugly, awful. What has happened here is simply tragic, outrageously evil. There is nothing good about it. Anyone who might try to pretend otherwise is out of touch with reality.
>
> Now that we've said that, now that we've acknowledged what we all know, let me share a

second thought, the only thing that makes any sense of our existence.

Only faith—by this I mean a personal relationship with Jesus Christ—is able to resurrect any meaning whatsoever from this or from our very lives.

They all had questions in relation to this event, from the youngest to the oldest, and even though the wording might be different, many were wondering:

Three days ago, these children were all here. We talked together, laughed together, played together. But today their desks are empty. Why are they gone? Why am I still here? Does life have any meaning at all? What is it all about, anyway?

Most who were in that audience knew that I was speaking from experience, sharing questions, thoughts and convictions that had been learned in the process of my own struggle with grief. Twenty-nine months earlier, just six months after moving to our new ministry, our own three-year-old son had died, following a sudden illness of undiagnosed origin.

His death began in me a prolonged struggle with these same issues. In that period, I had tried to maintain at least two things as constants. For one thing, I would not pretend, but tell the truth, facing head-on the pain and ugliness of death by calling it what it was. At the same time, I also looked for God to begin to make some sense of it all, bringing hope in the despair, meaning out of confusion and life out of loss at a time when it seemed that life had lost its joy.

In this period, while progressing through the normal grieving process with its anger and depression, I had also seen God's blessing on our ministry, as He was bringing to me a certain sensitivity and effectiveness that I could not have learned in the classroom.

At our son's funeral, I had claimed for us a passage from Isaiah:

> The Spirit of the Sovereign Lord is on me, because the Lord has anointed me to preach good news to the poor. He has sent me to bind up the brokenhearted . . . to comfort all who mourn . . . to bestow on them a crown of beauty instead of ashes, the oil of gladness instead of mourning, and a garment of praise instead of a spirit of despair.
>
> They will be called oaks of righteousness, a planting of the Lord for the display of his splendor (Isa. 61:1-3).

It was this last part, particularly, that seemed to be happening in relation to the deaths of the children and their mother. While I had not much strength in myself, the Lord had been strengthening and teaching me within, so that when the opportunity came for ministry in this very difficult setting, I had something to share that went beyond poems and prayers.

At the close of the school's memorial service, I was asked by the grieving father to speak at the funeral the next day. This was another significant opportunity, considering the history of relations between Catholics and

Protestants in those towns through the years. The preparation, though, brought some anxieties. What would the experience be like? How do you prepare a message for a mass funeral, a Catholic funeral?

The hall was full, and the mood somber as I sought to bring some healing in the midst of intense sorrow. That day, I think I was trying to reach out to that father, as much as to anyone. I expected that once the details were settled, he might face an extraordinary level of guilt and remorse, even despair.

I knew that, for me, the "if onlys" still might crowd my mind from time to time and that, in his case, they would probably be intensified. No one knew the origin of the fire, but the facts pointed to an overheated wood stove or an improperly cleaned chimney. It seemed that they had all died in their sleep, including the other family pets, except the one dog that had somehow escaped.

"If only I had been home," he might be thinking, as the parents had been separated for some time. "If only there had been a smoke detector. If only . . . "

The mortician and family had done their best to cosmetize things. The caskets were closed, of course, and there were lots of flowers and a picture of the victims on the appropriate caskets. But the whole front of the room was filled with caskets! You can't cosmetize a fact like that!

The situation was potentially overwhelming. Six caskets—how do you deal with that reality? It was like a scene from a horror story. If I let myself feel it, actually feel it, I'm not sure I would have been able to talk. But, as a pastor, sometimes you *have* to talk. So, as I talked, I was there in mind and spirit. But I think I was, again, partially disengaged in terms of emotions, although I cared especially about two things, reaching out to that grieving father and bearing witness to the truth of God:

> This scene before us, this experience is incredible; numbing—but *it is, sadly, true.* So we come in the face of such horror and we ask: *Can God help?* Does He know the way I feel? Can there be some consolation, some comfort to my aching heart? *Is He really there?* And, if He is—does He really care?

For me, these questions were not merely rhetorical in nature; the father knew that; the priest knew that; they all knew that. When the opportunity came to speak for God in that funeral home, He had given me something to say, a message of help and hope.

By then, many months of anguished struggling had given way to a new synthesis and a deeper faith, a synthesis not of my own doing, but the work of the Spirit of God, patiently leading me on to new meaning, when on one level, the joy of my life had been destroyed.

It was a synthesis of the temporal and eternal perspectives on reality. The temporal summary is, "We are all wasting away, day by day. Our life is as a vapor, here today, gone tomorrow. How can there be any significant meaning in it?"

The eternal affirms this first perspective, but offers a solution, "Now that you've realized your frailty, allow it to be caught up in My finality. Then your life can actually count for something eternally."

> Friends, family, if God cannot help, then faith is meaningless. Life is meaningless. And what we see before us here is like a grotesque

summary of the meaning of our existence. But, I truly believe, that it is precisely at these moments, moments of crisis, that God can . . . that God does intervene . . . He does step in and whisper, "I am here! I do care! I can and I will help you . . . if you really want Me to."

Jesus, I hurt! Nobody knows how bad I feel. Lord, I feel like I've been stuck by a knife—pierced by a spear in the heart—there's an empty, gaping hole in my life now. I feel like I've been set adrift in a little rowboat in an angry ocean and, any minute now, I'm going under. I don't know how much more I can take of this. God—if You are there—You have to help.

Looking back, the opportunity for ministry which arose from this tragedy was the most significant of my entire three and a half years in that community. In fact, I believe that God kept me there specifically to minister in that situation, despite my efforts to relocate. For months we had been seeking another place of service, without success. But when this tragedy occurred, because of my personal struggle with the same kinds of issues that now faced the students, community and church people, I realized the Lord had been preparing a message learned in life, rather than in the classroom setting.

In concluding the funeral remarks, I was still trying to give that father something of myself, a very personal message for the days I knew were coming:

Now, and especially after this is over, next week, next month, this will seem like a dark, dark cave—cold and dark, a passageway leading nowhere. And you may be groping for meaning, for a reason to continue, yes, even to live. When that happens, as it most surely will, *do not,* I beg you, *do not* try to fight it all by yourself, for it is much, much bigger than you are, and you will be destroyed. But if you will reach out to God, He will take your hand and guide you out of this darkness into His warm light again. I know He will.

Several years ago, following the death of a young boy, I wrote a poem to try to console his mother. Only a few months later, I discovered that I had to apply these words to myself. Perhaps they will be of help to you, as I read some of it:

ANSWERS PARTLY KNOWN
1 Corinthians 13:12

How quickly passed the years
From nursery to grave,
From fairy tales and rhymes,
And childhood hopes and fears.

So much unsaid, undone
So little time for toys
And joys, for plastic guns
And baseball games he won.

How slowly passed the hours,
How quietly the night,
Surrounded, yet alone,
'Mid faces, cards, and flowers.

So many questions press
Why him? Why here? Why now?
When will this numbness cease?
Where hope in this distress?

The mind seeks some relief,
Some answer that is clear.
In this, can God be near?
Does Jesus share my grief?

Through all the days that come,
To fill the emptiness,
Let Him provide the power
To live each lonely hour.
In darkness He is light,
The Morning after night.

The father seemed touched, and appreciative of my attempt to reach out to him. Although we didn't have much opportunity for interaction following that service, not long afterward he stopped by the parsonage with a gift for our little girl. Besides the family dog, there was one other survivor of the fire. It was a bicycle one of his children had owned, and now he wanted us to have it.

Over the past few days I had given of myself trying to meet that father's needs and the needs of others in this difficult situation. Now he was offering more than a plaything to our little girl—he was giving us something of himself, a vivid reminder of how God's ministry works both ways.

How Do *You* Identify?

How many times in your own lifetime will you lose someone to death you love very much? The answer probably depends upon how large your family is or how many close friendships you have cultivated over the years. As much as we try not to think about it, eventually it will happen. But no matter how many times we may be confronted by the death of a loved one, no doubt it will still be fewer times than what our pastors will be called upon in the next year to bury.

Having to deal with that much grief can eventually take its toll on any one of us. Most of us, in fact, avoid funeral homes and funeral services as if they were death themselves. None of us like to talk about death. People in our society no longer die, they "expire." Our friends who go into the hospitals with life-threatening illnesses are no longer considered so sick they will eventually die, rather we refer to them as being "terminal."

And yet, the fact remains that not everyone lives forever. Eventually people we know, people we love, people who are members of our church, will die. Some die in their sleep and others die in the midst of tragic circumstances. And in the face of this death and resulting grief, someone from the Church, namely the pastor, will be called upon to minister to those who have been touched by death. And this type of ministry is rarely ever easy.

Consider for a moment what is required to perform a funeral service for someone you may have never met. Not only must you prepare a service that in some manner relates to the life of the deceased, but also you must consider the variety of needs of the remaining family members. Much care is used in selecting appropriate passages of Scripture and much thought is given in order to meet everyone's needs. All of this takes time, involves the use of certain gifts and talents and is dependent upon a special sensitivity to the Holy Spirit.

And then consider the diffulty in preparing for a funeral where many members of one family have died, like our story, where there are six caskets all in a row.

What is it like when one must minister not only to the natural family, which is crushed by the loss brought upon by death, but also to the Church Body who make up the spiritual family. And then, what is it like when the one called to minister is crushed and needs to be ministered unto as well.

All of us, from time to time, will be called upon to deal with the death of a loved one. No doubt, this will be a time when we will need our pastor's loving support. Remember, this week or this month, your pastor will have to deal with the death of a member, or members, of his church family. There is no doubt that this will be a time when he will need your loving support.

13

The Cloning of a Pastor

Remade in *their* image was just what one church diaconate had in mind for their new pastor. Instead of allowing him to serve with his special blend of creative abilities and gifts for the ministry, they had their own plans for him. Who would win out? And who would end up pastoring the church, the pastor or the deacons?

Do you remember what your living room looked like the last time you moved? Boxes everywhere! How well I remember our move to a church I'll call Harmony Chapel. The moving van pulled away from the door of the parsonage; our work was cut out for us. A few days of emptying boxes and putting the house in order, and I would be ready to begin my duties at our new church.

But then the doorbell rang. We had been in the house

for not more than a half hour and our first visitor was already at the door. I thought maybe it was just the Welcome Wagon or a friendly neighbor stopping by to offer a helping hand, but that wasn't the case. It was one of our parishioners insisting that we meet with him at that very moment. We offered our guest the only chair we could find, and Jan and I made ourselves comfortable on a box of books.

Our guest did not blush when he came right to the point stating emphatically that the entire diaconate of Harmony Chapel should be dismissed. I was tempted to ask why, but better judgment prevailed. Instead, I asked the man for a reasonable period of time to get to know the members of the diaconate so that I could judge for myself. We agreed that three months would be a fair amount of time for me to get to know and consider the charges that had been made. Before we said good-bye to our guest, I suggested he take the time to write his grievances down, and he agreed to do so.

Mine may be the shortest pastoral honeymoon on record. On the first Monday following my arrival at Harmony Chapel, the church diaconate made a request that I meet with them for a planning session. I was about to find out for myself what our first guest at Harmony wanted to tell me about the diaconate.

As it turned out, the diaconate had some very promising ideas and plans for the future of Harmony Chapel. They had plans for a citywide evangelism program, they had plans for a Christian school and they had plans for their new pastor. Unfortunately, their plans for me were that I should become a carbon copy of each one of them.

Little did I know when my wife and I met with them weeks before our arrival that it was their plan for me to be molded, or better yet, cloned in their image. I left that first meeting excited about the opportunity to serve them with my creative abilities and gifts for the ministry. But I suspect they left like a bunch of mad scientists intent on cloning me in the image of how they believed the pastor should minister.

We came to Harmony Chapel at the request of our district superintendent. The church was without a pastor and was in need of someone to preach during the interim. That first Sunday at Harmony we were greeted by two members of the diaconate who requested we meet with the entire diaconate after the morning service for a time of fellowship and for some informal questions and answers. At this meeting, we discovered the church diaconate had some very promising ideas and plans for the future of their church. Quite frankly, I was so impressed with them that I agreed to their invitation to submit my name as a candidate to pastor Harmony Chapel. As we left the church that first weekend, Deacon Clay handed me a note on which he had written just one sentence, "You already have my vote."

After candidating the next week, we returned home and prayerfully waited. We did not have to wait long, for the call came at 9 A.M. the next morning, informing us that I had been called by the church to be their next pastor.

As I began to look into the charges leveled by that first guest, I recalled a few things I had learned about the recent past history of the church. Just prior to my coming, the church had experienced a split, and for three months the remaining group was left without a pastor. In an effort to heal the damage created by this split, the diaconate had begun to insist upon a sense of uniformity among the membership. Several of the members decided to conform to the wishes of the diaconate and, as a result, the diaconate's desire and need for power was fed and strengthened.

How sad it is to see how much the Church today is like the Corinthian Church, which lacked a sense of unity and yet insisted upon unity. Not only did the diaconate of Harmony Chapel desire that the congregation conform to their plans and vision for the church, but they had the same plan for the new pastor, whoever he might turn out to be. When I discovered their intent, I rebelled. If there is one thing a person in ministry must have, it is the freedom to obey God and his or her own understanding of Scripture, not the demands and desires of the diaconate who want to handle the pastor like a puppet on a string. I wasn't quite sure how I should react, but then decided to present a series of sermons and teachings on the book of First Corinthians, one which certainly allows for diversity within the bonds of unity.

Chapter 12 of 1 Corinthians has a single theme, namely, the need for diversity within the unity of the Church. In verse four, Paul says, "There are different kinds of gifts, but the same Spirit" (1 Cor. 12:4). Then Paul elaborates this point of diversity by numerating some of the spiritual gifts (vv 7-11).

Working from the presupposition that the human body functions with unity, Paul argues that not only is there room for diversity in the Church, but there must be a certain amount of diversity if the Body—the Church—is to function properly (vv. 12-17). Paul is not using this analogy to unite a church which is divided. He is, in fact, arguing quite the opposite, that there can be diversity within the bonds of unity. Paul underlines that fact by referring to the human body. We know that it is a single unit but, at the same time, it has many parts with different functions. The

Church is a single unit because of its one Spirit experience (1 Cor. 12:13) and yet, it too has many members, the individuals which make up the Church.

Throughout 1 Corinthians 12, Paul insists on diversity within the unity of the Body for, while the Corinthians were lacking in unity, they were insisting on uniformity. It has been said that imitation is the highest form of flattery. That may be true, but if the imitation is forced, if someone insists or demands that uniformity, then a motive must be sought.

In the case of the Corinthians, who insisted on uniformity, Paul seems to be saying that their motive was jealousy. Paul says that we should not deny the exercise of another's gift in the church, and if we do, it is because we are jealous of the fact that the other person may be exercising a more important gift than ours, a gift that we might not be capable of exercising (see 1 Cor. 12:22-24).

It was with this biblically-based belief that there is room for diversity within the Body that I began to meet those would-be "cloners" face-to-face. It was to be the kind of confrontation in which there would eventually be a winner and a loser. For me to win would be to retain my individuality, my personal style of ministry. For me to lose would be to end up in the mold of certain individuals on the diaconate and to become cloned in their images.

I remember reading once that when a pastor in the coal fields of the South wanted to say something against those members of the church who chewed tobacco, he would sometimes say something like, "Every time they open their mouth, their brains dribble off the end of their chins." I've often thought that was a good description of one of my would-be cloners, Deacon Dibble.

Deacon Dibble was a Sunday School teacher as well as

a deacon and had decided that it would be well for the church if I patterned my teaching methods after his. So, with that in mind, I sat in on a few of Dibble's classes and I listened to him dribble. One of those lessons had to do with the resurrection of Jesus (I think). I listened as carefully as I could and came away from the lesson, how should I say it, amazed.

Listening to Dibble was like being out in the middle of the Pennsylvania Dutch country, where people speak English but with German sentence structure, something like "Throw me down the stairs, please, my hat." Or, "The man threw his grandmother out the window of the train, a kiss." That's exactly how Dibble delivered his discourse on the resurrection. Actually, it sounded a great deal like our nine-year-old daughter who returned home from school one day to announce that she had just learned that, "It is 93,000,000 miles from the earth to the sun, but the sun is really a lot farther away than that."

Shortly thereafter, I met another would-be cloner, Deacon Tottle, the teetotaler. Tottle was the self-proclaimed, all-around, church expert. What Tottle did not know about any biblical subject was not worth knowing, and he did not mind saying so. In fact, it was Tottle's new goal in life to tell me everything I needed to know about pastoral ministry. He tried to tell me what to preach, how to preach it and when to preach it. He had his own idea of what a pastor was to be like and he was determined to clone me into that image, his own image.

I may be expressing the sentiments of a number of pastors when I say that I find it more than just interesting that it is particularly in the field of religion that so many want to come across as experts. When someone goes for medical attention they may ask the doctor to tell them the cure, but when it comes to religion and the pastoral minis-try, few ask, because most everyone already presumes to know the answers.

I am not saying that all pastors know everything there is to know about the Bible, but in many cases, he or she has had more biblical training than anyone else in the church. That's why the church called them to fill the pulpit and to perform pastoral duties. So why is it so difficult for some people to acknowledge that their pastor is the theologian, teacher and minister-in-residence?

Deacon Tottle did his best to mold me into his image of what a pastor should be and, in fact, pastor the church himself through me. But it just didn't work. In order to have harmony you must have different notes played in their proper order. If the notes fall in the wrong order, the result is discord because the notes clash. There was a clash between Deacon Tottle and myself. The sad thing was that not only was Tottle out of order in his attempts to clone me in his own image, but I began to detect some hints that his life was out of order.

One night I received a telephone call with a voice saying, "Please come quickly, it's Tottle, he's very sick." I rushed to his home and found him crouched in a corner crying out, "Stay away from me! Stay away from me!" For several years, teetotaler Tottle had been tipping the bottle and was now beginning to see imaginary snakes crawling around his living room.

We were able to persuade Tottle to go for help and for awhile he seemed to improve. But a few weeks later, Tottle was back on the bottle and this time, he came out of the closet with his drinking. His drinking became worse than ever and his attitude and disposition worsened. We encouraged Tottle to seek help once again but this time he would not acknowledge his problem; he turned us down and tuned us out.

Life teaches us that there are some things that simply will not go away by ignoring them. On the other hand, there are some things which will, and Tottle's wife was one of them. She divorced her husband, and soon after Tottle left Harmony Chapel and went the way of the world.

I have often asked myself the question, "Where did I go wrong in trying to help Tottle?" Could I have done more toward preventing his divorce and helping him with his drinking problem? As a pastor, I feel some personal responsibility for the domestic and spiritual lives of those whom I shepherd. But in Tottle's case, did I allow his attempts to dominate me and clone me stand in the way of my ability and desire to minister to him? For all those who are hurting, be informed that your pastor is hurting too.

Deacon Clay, another member of Harmony Chapel's diaconate, was the "model deacon." He was the kind of leader who was always out front pointing the way. He led the way when it came to mowing the church lawn. He led the way in deciding the spiritual direction of Harmony Chapel. He led the way in deciding who would be granted membership in the church. In fact, there was not a single thing about Harmony Chapel in which Deacon Clay did not lead the way, including his efforts to control and dominate the life of the pastor. It was his greatest desire in life that I should be, in a sense, *his* pastoral assistant. If he couldn't clone me, he wanted to pull all my strings.

To be a leader like Deacon Clay might at first seem like a commendable thing, that is, until you realize that Clay not only led the way but *wanted* his way in everything. I soon found out that Clay was the senior member of the diaconate and was honorably recognized as a leader by the other members of the board. I was soon to find out just how much power that "recognition" entailed.

Harmony Chapel was about to undergo some remodeling which required the purchase of $700 worth of new building material. As usual, Clay was in charge, so he ordered the materials, picked them up and stored them in a back room of the church basement. The church fell behind in its remodeling schedule and the work which required the new materials was postponed until the arrival of spring. However, for some reason known only to Deacon Clay, possibly due to our failure to keep to our remodeling schedule, the material was removed from the room and placed outdoors behind the church.

The snow finally melted, warm weather arrived and the remodeling of the church was back on schedule. The work crew searched throughout the building for the materials and finally found them out-of-doors. Unfortunately, the winter had taken its toll; the materials had been ruined and the church was out $700. A quick inquiry revealed who was at fault and Deacon Clay was asked to come before the diaconate and give an account of his actions. Clay readily admitted that he had stacked the stuff outside because of the clutter it made in a room which could have been used for a Sunday School class. I was about to ask Deacon Clay a further question when he stated that if we did not give him the right to do as he pleased, when he pleased, and give him the right to buy and handle matters as he saw fit, then he would resign from the diaconate.

It was hard to believe what happened next. One of the deacons actually brought that question to a vote and Deacon Clay won, five to one. A few days later, however, they reconsidered their vote. A special meeting of the diaconate was called by Deacon Ritter to consider whether or not they really wanted Deacon Clay to have that much authority. The diaconate took a vote and reversed their previous decision. Deacon Clay resigned from the diaconate. One week later he left the church and went his separate way.

How quickly we forget that Christ asks us for a constant reaffirmation of our commitment, not only to Him but to the Body as well. Sometimes we perceive discipleship to be a one-time declaration, an allegiance pledged at a point in time, usually in years past. However, Jesus said that we are to take up our cross daily and follow Him or we cannot be His disciple (see Luke 14:27). There must be therefore, a regular renewal of the unconditional giving of ourselves to Jesus, to be molded into *His* image, not cloned in the image of one another.

More than three months had passed since we arrived at Harmony Chapel and we had not yet talked with our first Harmony guest. Of course, he had not pushed to keep our three-month appointment, for he was quite pleased at seeing the various members of the diaconate resign.

The day finally did come when we sat down to talk and once again our guest got straight to the point. He presented what he considered to be evidence demonstrating that the entire diaconate of Harmony Chapel was in one way or another unfit to hold their offices of deacon.

Since that occasion, I have thought about the implications of this problem as it exists at Harmony Chapel and, I suspect, in other churches as well. What does the pastor or the church body as a whole do when it appears that certain members who are elected to office may not be qualified to hold that office? What is the pastor and church body to do when certain individuals in leadership positions seek to mold, influence or clone the pastor in their own image that they might retain and increase their hold of power on the church?

I am serving as pastor in a geographical area where five churches in the past two years have been disgraced and divided by their own diaconates. Those five churches now exist with an advisory board but not a diaconate. Could it be that the Church is not a democracy and therefore does not need a diaconate? Is the Church a theocracy in need of only a spiritual guide, a shepherd, a pastor?

What then, is the answer? I believe that it is in our willingness to recognize that others have been gifted for ministry according to their own personalities and strengths and that they might best minister if released to serve in their areas of expertise. Discord results when members of the Body desire or are asked to serve on boards, committees or in positions for which they are not gifted.

Once again we turn to chapter 12 of 1 Corinthians and Paul's analogy of the Church as a Body. To say that the Church does not need the input of the lay person in the role of deacon would be to deny the analogy and the book of Acts. To place either the pastor as sole leader or to attempt to clone him in the image of any other individual would be to deny the diversity of gifts that God has given to the Church, whereby the Body might be edified and equipped for service.

How Do *You* Identify?

In the May 17, 1985 issue of *Christianity Today,* Marshall Shelley concludes an article on "The Problem of Battered Pastors,"[1] by offering three suggestions which could be used by pastors and lay persons in recognizing and releasing one another to use their God-given gifts for the benefit of the Church. In summary, his suggestions are:

1. *Look for gifts, not greatness.* Both congregations and pastors are looking for individuals to serve the Church, but let's not cause problems by looking for "supermen" and "superwomen." God has gifted the whole Body so that together we might turn the world upside down for Christ. There are few people who are gifted and talented enough to accomplish that task in and of themselves.

2. *Let the pastor lead with personal strengths.* Each pastor has special gifts and should be allowed to "major" in those areas. The problem comes when we expect the pastor to be skilled in or to favor an area of ministry that might be special to us or in which we have been gifted. And when he isn't, we are tempted to squeeze him into our mold, to clone him in our image. And pastors, the same applies to you. Not every member of the congregation has the same gifts that you might have and should not be expected to function with the same intensity and skill as you in every area of ministry.

3. *Let commitment mean something.* Three deacons left Harmony Chapel. Instead of being willing to face the conflict, they left. Just think how strong the Church would be, how much Harmony Chapel and your church could accomplish for the Lord, if people who disagreed were willing to struggle together to work out their differences instead of running away from them.

Afterword

Is the story of your life like ours? That shouldn't be so surprising, after all. For one thing, we are people, too, like you, with similar strengths and weaknesses, hopes and dreams. For another, our lives are intertwined with yours, not only as pastors and parishioners, but more significantly as brothers and sisters in the family of God.

Unlike any other army, we Christian soldiers tend to shoot our wounded. We not only must stop the shooting, but, as the family of God, make a crucial commitment to one another to begin bringing healing, understanding, cooperation and love to each other. Remember, we're in this together.

At first glance, the selection of stories included in this volume might seem rather dramatic. In reality, however, they are no more or less dramatic than the life experiences occurring around us everyday. How many times a day—nationwide—for instance, does someone write off years of marriage with the words, "I've fallen in love with someone else." Or, how many thousands are grappling with the heart-wrenching issue of euthanasia, or mental illness, alcoholism or betrayal?

Do you know anyone who is wrestling with knowing God's will regarding the call of a pastor—or any other major decision? Perhaps you've personally struggled with criticism and rejection, conformity to someone else's mold, or low self-esteem. If so, welcome to the club—the "people in process" club, as one of our friends put it while reflecting on this material.

The point is, none of us has yet arrived. Instead, like Paul whose single-minded purpose was, "Forgetting what is behind and straining toward what is ahead, I press on toward the goal to win the prize for which God has called me heavenward in Christ Jesus" (Phil. 3:13-14).

In truth, God has called all of us heavenward. Therefore, we are involved in a lifelong process of growth in godliness, as we move toward the ultimate prize of hearing, "Well done, good and faithful servant!" (Matt. 25:23).

Just as we share a mutual calling, we also share a mutual ministry, serving others in the name of Christ. Too often, the work of the ministry has been left to the clergy—the paid professionals—instead of being shared among those God has equipped and gifted to have a part and even to lead in certain areas *instead of* the paid professionals.

It is difficult to imagine anyone so gifted that he or she may be an expert in dealing with all of the life experiences represented in these pages. Yet, sometimes, just such an expectation is held of the pastor—either by the church, community or even by himself. The problem, of course, is that this expectation is unreasonable, simply because that person is human and just as subject to the same weaknesses and limitations of body, soul and spirit, as everyone else.

This expectation, besides being unreasonable, is also contrary to God's plan for the functioning of the Church—the priesthood of believers—in which all are called and equipped for the work of service, so the Body of Christ will be built up in faith, hope and love. Everyone has an important part in this ministry, functioning according to the grace of God and using the gifts of God, with the result being a wonderful unity in diversity, which is itself a reflection of the character of God. Yes, you are important. God can use even you in the ministry!

Our hope is that by interacting with these glimpses of our lives several things will have happened:

1. You will have developed a greater appreciation of your importance as a member of God's ministry team. Being faithful to our upward calling involves obedient service, not sainthood, while responding in the given ministry setting with the creativity and flexibility that comes from dependence on the Spirit of God. One important result we hope for is an increasing sense of support, understanding and love of all the ministers—clergy and otherwise—for one another as we labor in the same vineyard for the same Lord.

2. You will have received help when facing situations similar to those described here. While we do not present our stories as paragons of perfection and worthy of imitation, we do hope that in them you have discerned certain principles which, having helped us, will likewise help you.

3. You will have found hope, especially if you are presently facing a situation similar to one of those just described. None of the writers offers a three-step plan for victory. But we trust it will be encouraging to know that

we can all derive strength from knowing that we serve a Lord who identifies with us because He walked in our shoes.

You can also take courage that there are others—pastors, in this case—who have likewise grappled with issues close to your heart—not only surviving, but serving effectively today, often because of and not in spite of the difficulties that have come our way.

God bless you!

Notes

Chapter 1

1. From: *The Right to Live The Right to Die.* By: C. Everett Koop. Published by Tyndale House Publishers, Inc. © 1976. Used by permission.
2. Paul Ramsey, "On Dying Well," *Ethics at the Edge of Life* (New Haven, CT: Yale University Press, 1978), p. 150.
3. Thomas Elkins, "A Legacy of Life," in *Christianity Today* 29 (January 18, 1985), p. 25.

Chapter 3

1. From *Magnificent Marriage* by Gordon MacDonald. © 1980 Tyndale House Publishers, Inc. Used by permission.

Chapter 7

1. "Onward Christian Soldiers," Sabine Baring-Gould, 1834-1924, public domain.

Chapter 13

1. Marshall Shelley, "The Problems of Battered Pastors," *Christianity Today* (May 1985), pp. 34-37.